DATE DUE

SOCIAL INNOVATION, INC.

SOCIAL

INNOVATION, INC.

5 STRATEGIES FOR DRIVING
BUSINESS GROWTH
THROUGH SOCIAL CHANGE

JASON SAUL

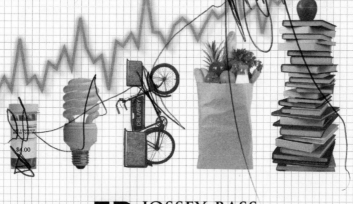

JB **JOSSEY-BASS**
A Wiley Imprint
www.josseybass.com

Published by Jossey-Bass
A Wiley Imprint
989 Market Street, San Francisco, CA 94103-1741— www.josseybass.com

Jossey-Bass books and products are available through most bookstores. To contact Jossey-Bass directly call our Customer Care Department within the U.S. at 800-956-7739, outside the U.S. at 317-572-3986, or fax 317-572-4002.

Jossey-Bass also publishes its books in a variety of electronic formats. Some content that appears in print may not be available in electronic books.

Library of Congress Cataloging-in-Publication Data
Saul, Jason, 1969-
  Social innovation, Inc. : 5 strategies for driving business growth through social change / Jason Saul.
     p. cm.
  Includes index.
    ISBN 978-0-470-61450-1 (hardback)
  1. Social responsibility of business. 2. Social entrepreneurship. 3. Strategic planning. 4. Social change—Economic aspects. I. Title.
    HD60.S267 2010
    658.4'063—dc22

                                                                                      2010024713

Printed in the United States of America
FIRST EDITION
HB Printing   10 9 8 7 6 5 4 3 2 1

To my wife, Lisa, who innovated the ultimate social change in my life: our two children, Jonah and Max Julius

Contents

Introduction

There are three ways to change the world: change
China, change California, or change Walmart.
                          —*William McDonough, architect, designer,*
                                              and sustainability expert

W almart has figured out how to turn a profit by selling just
about anything. From horse shampoo to sliced cactus to
yarn ball winders, Walmart can make dimes out of dust: 2008
net profits were more than $12 billion. But there is one thing
Walmart has yet to make profitable: doing good. Which is not
to say it doesn't do a lot of good: In 2009, Walmart Stores Inc.
and its affiliates gave $423 million in cash and in-kind gifts to
charity around the world, provided more than 100 million pounds
of food to U.S. food banks, and volunteered more than one million
volunteer hours.[1] But, from a business standpoint, the 100,000
plus charities that Walmart supports are cash outlays with no clear
return on investment. Now, as social issues like the environment,
education, health care, and global development become critical
to business success, Walmart and companies like it are asking the
question: *How do we turn social strategies into business strategies?*

At Walmart headquarters, the writing was on the wall. *Literally.*
In the lobby of the Walmart home office in Bentonville, Arkansas,
the walls are lined with plaques commemorating key milestones
in the company's history. 2006 marked a particularly important
milestone: it was the year Walmart announced its $4 prescription
drug program, a program that guaranteed all Walmart customers
access to most generic prescription drugs at only $4. Since its incep-
tion, the program has generated more than $2 billion in savings

for Walmart customers, particularly the uninsured and Medicare recipients.[2] Moreover, the "Walmart effect" has prompted other big pharmacies like CVS and Walgreens to follow suit, lowering health care costs across the board. The business impact has been tremendous: from September 21 to November 12, 2006, when the program was rolled out to the first twenty-seven states, 2.1 million more new prescriptions were filled by Walmart in those states compared to the same time periods in the prior year.[3] Indeed, the $4 generic program has catapulted Walmart to become the nation's third-largest pharmacy, with 16 percent market share,[4] and demand for $4 medicines helped spur growth of its U.S. comparable-stores sales by 3.3 percent in 2008.[5]

What makes the $4 prescription so extraordinary is that it was designed as *business strategy*. Yet its social impact is potentially greater than any philanthropic effort could ever produce. *Could Walmart possibly offer a better solution to health care than Medicaid?* And if so ...

- Could IBM educate students better than charter schools?

- Could GE help reduce global warming faster than the Kyoto protocol?

- Could Starbucks do more to stabilize the economy in Rwanda than U.S. foreign aid?

I wrote this book to answer these questions and to teach companies how to turn social change into a powerful business strategy. There have been many books about how businesses can "do well by doing good." This is not one of them. Rather, this is a book about corporate strategy. It is based on more than four years of research measuring the corporate responsibility and philanthropy for many of America's largest corporations. The data made one thing very clear: very few of these programs generated any measurable business value. Most were designed for a very different purpose: doing good. But there were a few strategies that stood out—true business strategies that happened to involve positive social change as a leverage point. These strategies produced breakthrough business results by *solving social problems*. Some involved creating new socially impactful products and services, like the $4 generic drug program or low-cost health insurance for young people. Other innovations served unmet needs in ignored or hard-to-reach markets, like urban "food deserts" or extremely poor countries. Some companies innovated alternative solutions to public education by building their own "talent pipeline." And some companies were able to create powerful, emotional bonds with customers by using their core business to solve social problems, like preventing tetanus for pregnant moms and newborn children. Finally, I came across companies that turned governments into business partners: working in innovative ways with public officials to solve social problems in ways that also drive business results, like soap companies educating children about hygiene, or technology companies investing in innovations that increase access to health care. These strategies are what I call *social innovations*, and they offer the keys to unlocking the potential of one of the last great untapped business markets: society.

Today, companies are operating in a totally different economic context: a market where social change has economic value. Former vice president Al Gore said, "Your employees, your colleagues, your board, your investors, your customers are all soon going to place a much higher value—and the markets will soon place a much higher value—on an assessment of how much you are a part of the solution to these [social] issues."[6] Leading companies are realizing that in order to succeed, they must figure out how to design, manufacture, and sell a product called social impact. Unfortunately, most corporations turn their business brains off when they think about social issues. Most corporate social strategies, from grants to volunteering to environmental auditing, were designed to satisfy society's expectations, not to create business value. This book teaches you how to turn your business brain back on, to create a new generation of social strategies *designed* to drive business growth.

Social Innovation, Inc. is written in three sections. Part I, The New Economics of Social Change, sets the context for a new way of thinking about social change. It details the drivers of the social capital market and evidence for its strength, the wide chasm between corporate social responsibility and true business strategy, and how social innovation strategies drive value. Part II, Five Strategies for Corporate Social Innovation, details each of the five social innovation strategies, showing how to create revenues with submarket products and services, enter new markets through backdoor channels, build emotional bonds with customers, develop new pipelines for talent, and influence policy through reverse lobbying. Each chapter begins with an illustrative case study of a company that has successfully implemented the social innovation strategy, and continues with a detailed explanation of how the strategy works, the trends that made it possible, and the tips you'll need to be successful. Part III, The Roadmap to Social Innovation focuses on the practical realities of crafting and implementing social innovation strategies. This includes explaining how companies can create an enabling environment for social innovation, walking through the steps needed to determine the right social innovation strategy and how to integrate it with the business and measure social and business impact, and offering insights about the implications of social innovation for socially responsible investors, government policymakers, and nonprofits.

This book is about corporate strategy, not corporate responsibility. It is designed to help companies elevate their social strategies beyond moral obligations, to generate real business value through positive social change. It is written for those who run companies and those who seek to influence companies. If you believe that social issues have real economic consequences, then it becomes imperative for your company to forge social strategies into business strategies. This book will show you how.

SOCIAL
INNOVATION, INC.

Part I

THE NEW ECONOMICS
OF SOCIAL CHANGE

Until recently, when companies looked at society, all they saw were costs and risks: regulations, taxes, lawsuits, complaints, grant requests. Activists protest and boycott companies to expose other "hidden" costs, such as globalization, discrimination, ozone depletion, animal testing, and human rights violations. Economists call these costs "externalities." Policymakers develop regulations and taxes to force companies to internalize the costs of these externalities. And the market discounts or "prices" certain externalities into the value of a business. All of this reinforces the view that for business, society only shows up on one side of the balance sheet.

Although these costs aren't going away (in fact, they're probably getting even bigger, as the 2010 BP oil leak in the Gulf of Mexico vividly demonstrates), businesses are now beginning to see the "hidden" economic *benefits* of solving intractable problems facing society. The famed bottom of the pyramid is just the tip of the economic iceberg. Embracing the business potential of issues like the environment, education, health care, hunger relief, discrimination, and economic development could earn companies tens of billions of dollars, open up new markets, attract new customers, prompt new innovations, and dramatically lower costs. I refer to this unrealized market potential as "social arbitrage." Indeed, the economic value of social change (by investors, employees, customers, and consumers) has given birth to an entirely new market: a *social capital market*.

To capitalize on this new market potential, companies will need to transcend the current mind-set around compliance and responsibility and focus on value creation. The following chapters set forth the context (and logic) for a fundamentally different approach to the business of social change.

Chapter 1

THE RISE OF THE SOCIAL
CAPITAL MARKET

*The current economic crisis does not represent just
another economic cycle; it represents a fundamental
reset ... an emotional, social, economic reset.*[1]

—*Jeffrey Immelt, CEO of General Electric*

Social issues always used to be an afterthought for corporations.
Businesses focused first on making money; then, once bills were
paid and profits booked, they looked for ways to "give back." That's
because, as Milton Friedman always said, the business of business
is business. And for most corporations, this will always be true. But
the *business* of business is changing, in large part because issues
previously considered "soft," like the environment, education,
health care, and global development, now have hard economic
impacts. Indeed, when it comes to making key economic decisions,
mainstream investors, consumers, CEOs, employees, the media, and
Wall Street increasingly value social and environmental impacts.
It said a lot when, in 2009, financial data giant Bloomberg decided
to include environmental, social, and governance information
(ESG) on 2,000-plus companies for clients using their 250,000
data terminals.

This new economic reality has completely transformed the role
of business in society (and the role of society in business). Today,

corporate success increasingly depends on social change. Think about it: companies across sectors cannot grow without tapping into underserved "social" markets like the uninsured, urban food deserts, or giant developing economies like India. Companies cannot take advantage of these new markets without developing "social" products and services. Companies cannot hire the talent they need, especially in developing countries, without improving educational opportunities for young people. And companies cannot build brand loyalty without a social or emotional bond to the customer. These are all characteristics of a new economy—a *social capital market* that attaches economic value to social change. To maximize growth and profits, companies have to understand the magnitude of this social capital market in which they operate, its drivers, and all its implications for them. Simply put, social change has become a valuable economic commodity: people are willing to pay for it, sacrifice for it, invest in it, and work for it. As a result, corporations are desperately trying to figure out how to produce it.

Does that mean companies have to sacrifice profits in order to do good? Quite the opposite. *Because* the market now values social impact, companies are no longer expected to be purely altruistic. In other words, it's okay to use social change as a business strategy. Venture capitalists invest in renewable-energy companies mostly because they're expecting outsized returns—that they're good for the environment is more or less a bonus. Electronics giant Siemens AG earned 17 billion euros in 2007 (nearly 25 percent of its revenues) from environmental and climate-related products like wastewater reuse systems and CO_2 abatement products.[2] We as consumers are part of this trend too: we purchase hybrid cars not just to show solidarity for the environment, but *also* to protect our wallets when gas prices are high; we use websites like kiva.org to make microloans to poor entrepreneurs and get our money back (in some cases, even *with interest*). In each of these instances, corporations and people are driven by *a compelling economic motive* to make positive social change. Indeed, through creative market mechanisms like these, corporations, consumers, and investors are finding ways to value social change beyond mere tax incentives and psychic benefits.

Size of the Social Capital Market

Indicators of the social capital market's size are everywhere you look—and many places you may not. Consumers are putting unprecedented numbers of hybrids and other fuel-saving cars on the road. The number of articles in major magazines and newspapers about biofuels, solar power, or any kind of up-and-coming alternative energy is soaring. Overall, U.S. consumers are estimated to spend over $220 billion annually on goods and services related to health, the environment, social justice, and sustainable living; this market comprises sixty-three million consumers, or 30 percent of the U.S. market.[3]

It's no surprise that companies are investing heavily to capture a piece of the social capital market, spending a combined $32 billion annually on environmental sustainability, governance, risk, compliance, social responsibility, and philanthropy.[4] The social capital market is also driving increasingly significant profits with products that promote positive social and environmental change: as mentioned earlier, Siemens AG derives almost 25 percent of its revenues from environment-related products, and GE's *ecomagination* strategy generated more than $17 billion in 2008 from eco-innovations in wind turbines, water desalination, and other areas.[5]

The social and environmental dimension of the investment industry is booming. There are 260 socially screened mutual fund products in the United States, with assets of $201.8 billion. A total of $2.71 trillion in the United States (and about $6.8 trillion globally[6]) is invested more broadly in various funds, pensions, trusts, and other vehicles that use one or more of the three core socially responsible investing (SRI) strategies—screening, shareholder advocacy, and community investing.[7] What is most interesting, though, is that the fastest-growing area of SRI is community investing. Over the past decade, community investing—putting money into underserved communities as an investment strategy—has grown an astounding 540 percent, from $4 billion to $25.8 billion in assets.[8] The investments earn competitive returns, but also produce an attractive social return by giving lower-income people access to capital, credit, and training in communities that lack affordable housing, child care, health care, and jobs that pay a living wage.[9]

Where is all this money coming from, and why? According to the European Social Investment Forum, there are four key drivers: an increasing demand from institutional investors, for which responsible investment becomes a matter of risk management, particularly around the area of climate change; a further mainstreaming of environmental, social, and governance (ESG) considerations into traditional financial services; external pressure from nonprofits and the media; and a growing interest from individuals, particularly the wealthy.[10]

The Dow Jones Industrial Average now has its own socially responsible twin, the Dow Jones Sustainability World Index (DJSWI), which comprises several different indices based on the top 10 percent of companies driving sustainability worldwide. The DJSWI grew over 36 percent in 2009.[11] Not to be outdone, Goldman Sachs, still one of the most venerated Wall Street firms and a survivor of the recent financial services collapse, has developed its own index, called GS SUSTAIN, which outperformed the market by 25 percent by incorporating ESG data.[12] Late 2009 saw the formation of the Global Impacting Investing Network (GIIN), a public-private partnership supported by J.P. Morgan, Citigroup, the United States Agency for International Development (USAID), and the Rockefeller Foundation, among others. The GIIN's charter is to develop a better industry infrastructure, along with enhanced metrics and reporting standards, for socially responsible investing. It's another clear indicator of the growing social capital market.[13]

It's hard to say just how big the social capital market is, given its broad contours and dynamism. By several estimates, it represents a many-trillion-dollar business opportunity, with just the purchasing power of the bottom of the pyramid (that is, the world's poorest populations) alone estimated at $5 trillion; such realities are motivating corporate giants like Microsoft and a host of others to view "inequity as a business problem as well as something to be addressed through philanthropy."[14] Thus for today's companies, it's not a question of whether to engage in this market, but how. To answer that, we have to understand the primary drivers behind the social capital market, or what we'll call the "SCM" in this book.

Drivers of the Social Capital Market

The SCM didn't appear overnight. It has been developing and maturing over the last thirty years, driven by social, economic, and political forces converging to make SCM one of the largest and most powerful markets ever seen. Here are five major drivers that made the SCM possible.

1. Corporations Are More Powerful Than Governments

Eric Schlosser notes in his book *Fast Food Nation*, "The McDonald's Corporation has become a powerful symbol of America's service economy, which is now responsible for 90 percent of the country's new jobs."[15] Each year McDonald's hires about one million people, more than any other American organization, public or private. An estimated one out of every eight workers in the United States has been employed by the fast-food franchiser at some point. McDonald's is the largest owner of retail property in the world,[16] and now feeds a record twenty-seven million Americans every day—forty-seven million globally. Numbers aside, McDonald's has also become the new civic hub in many communities, hosting fundraisers, sponsoring sports teams, providing scholarships, building parks, and even offering kid-friendly workout facilities.

The sheer economic power of corporations highlights their influence today. Indeed, fifty-one of the world's one hundred largest "economies" are now corporations.[17] Case in point: in 2007, Finland's budget was about 40 billion euros, 20 percent less than Nokia's annual sales.[18] Corporations are making more, spending more, and employing more of the world's resources than ever before. In the United States alone, total revenues for the Fortune 500 in 2005 hit $9.1 trillion, which is 73 percent of U.S. GDP.[19] Al Gore put it this way: "More money is allocated by markets around the world in one hour than by all the governments on the planet in a full year."[20]

Because of trends like these, business now plays a significantly larger role in our daily lives than does government; that also means companies are better positioned than federal and local governments to understand and address consumers' needs in a variety of areas. And we fully expect them to. The public is increasingly looking to corporations to solve social problems: 89 percent of consumers believe that corporate obligations to shareholders must be balanced by contributions to the broader public good—for example, providing good jobs, making philanthropic donations, and going beyond legal requirements to minimize pollution and other negative effects of business activities.[21] Corporate managers have heard the message: six out of ten executives believe that the public expects companies to take just as much responsibility as governments do for handling social issues.[22]

Corporations and for-profit social enterprises are responding to this call to action, and quickly. In many ways, business is moving faster than government to solve social problems. Look at the Chicago Climate Exchange. Well before the U.S. government got its act together on a cap-and-trade system, corporations banded together to create a voluntary marketplace for self-imposed carbon emissions. Companies like Walmart and WellPoint, the nation's largest health insurer, have been reducing the number of U.S. uninsured faster and cheaper than the U.S. government by using business innovations. The MTV cable network was better able to raise awareness and increase prevention of human trafficking in Asia and the Pacific than any government agency—reaching 380 million households through its MTV EXIT documentary.[23] These trends are likely to amplify, as corporations continue to get bigger, move faster, and connect more closely to our everyday lives.

2. Consumers Are More Powerful Than Citizens

If corporations are stronger than government now, it's no surprise that consumers wield more influence with their purchases and investments than citizens do with their votes. In his book *Supercapitalism*, economist Robert Reich, secretary of labor for the Clinton administration, argues that fast-moving technology and other factors have made capitalism "triumphant" and democracy "enfeebled," granting unprecedented power to corporate executives, growth-obsessed shareholders and investors, and consumers accustomed to the highest number of product choices ever. Even the most civic-minded among us cast political ballots only about once a year, on average, but we vote with our pocketbooks daily, increasingly choosing to buy organic products, green household cleaners, and socially responsible investment vehicles—we've become more powerful as consumers than as citizens. Because we're typically willing to pay more for social-values-based products, companies don't have to internalize their costs; they just have to make those products available. And when Walmart chooses to make more sustainable or organic products available, so does everyone else.

There's even a name for the movement toward social-values-based products and services. LOHAS is the acronym for Lifestyles of Health and Sustainability, and according to lohas.com, it's a "market segment focused on health and fitness, the environment, personal development, sustainable living, and social justice." In other words, it advocates purchases and activities that promote positive social and environmental change.

So Lohasians, as they're called, are into organic apples and shirts, green building supplies and stocks, and ecotourism, among many other goods and services. This is far from a niche segment; by some estimates, LOHAS comprises sixty-three million consumers, or 30 percent of the U.S. market, with $227 billion in annual spend.[24] Lohasians spend up to a 20-percent premium on clean, green products over nonsustainable alternatives. These consumers are nearly twice as likely to associate their own personal values with companies and their brands, and research shows that perceptions of environmental, ethical, and social stewardship are the fastest-growing influencers of consumer brand value.

3. Social Issues Are Now Business Issues

In a recent survey by McKinsey & Co., CEOs were asked, "Which of the following global environmental, social and political issues are the most critical to address for the future success of your business?" Here's what they found:

- Fifty percent of CEOs chose "educational systems, talent constraints."
- Forty-four percent chose "poor public governance."
- Thirty-eight percent chose "climate change."
- Thirty-six percent chose "making globalization's benefits accessible to the poor" (for example, bottom-of-the-pyramid product development and marketing, microfinance).
- Thirty-five percent chose "security of energy supply."
- Twelve percent chose "access to clean water, sanitation."
- Eight percent chose "HIV/AIDS and other public health issues."[25]

One hundred percent of respondents named a social issue that was directly affecting the success of their businesses; no one wrote in, "not applicable." The very fact that McKinsey is conducting this survey says a lot about the growing importance of social issues in business. The bottom line: social issues are no longer optional for today's business leaders. Here's a closer look at why that is the case.

Environment

The global population uses over 320 billion kilowatt hours of energy a day, or the equivalent of twenty-two light bulbs burning for twenty-four hours for every person on the planet.[26] We're expected to use about three times that much within the next century. Fossil fuels are finite, and they contribute to problems like pollution and global warming. Almost no one questions these facts now. Energy is a big problem—and big problems require big solutions.

The companies that generate big solutions to the big problems—whether with wind, solar panels, hydrogen cells, or other technologies to provide alternative energy or decrease the impact of fossil fuels—are going to drive the greatest profits, and the greatest environmental benefits. Among them is GE, who is leading the way with its *ecomagination* strategy: innovating products like locomotive emissions kits (that reduce pollution associated with train operations), amorphous transformers (more efficient, lower-CO_2-emitting transformers used in electric grids), desalination technologies (to convert saltwater to freshwater), and other energy-efficient solutions that contributed to more than $17 billion in revenues in 2008.[27] The *ecomagination* website sums it up: "Through *ecomagination*, we're helping to solve the world's biggest environmental challenges while driving profitable growth for GE." Clearly, GE understands that social and environmental issues are potentially very profitable business issues.

Education

The unfortunate reality is that most corporations are directly paying the price for America's education woes. Despite enormous investments in education (U.S. federal and state governments will spend more than $540 billion in 2011[28]), high school dropout rates are still unacceptably high and the United States placed near the bottom among Organisation for Economic Co-operation and Development (OECD) nations on math and science skills. As a result, companies can no longer count on the U.S. education system to produce students with the skills they need to succeed in the modern workplace. So it's not surprising that private companies are helping to create "alternative educational pathways" to foster the skills they need (discussed extensively in Chapter Seven: Develop New Pipelines for Talent). Such pathways include career academies funded by corporations and private-sector apprenticeships. Higher-quality vocational schools and online learning options are also helping to address the skills gaps.

Solving the education problem also presents a tremendous business opportunity for corporations. According to the Education Industry Association, education is rapidly becoming a $1 trillion industry, representing 10 percent of America's GNP and second in size only to the health care industry.[29] Education companies alone generate more than $80 billion in annual revenues.[30] The for-profit market includes everything from child care and pre-kindergarten spending, testing and training, technology, post-secondary education, and trade schools. Education, both as an issue and as an opportunity, is economically significant.

Health Care

The growing attention to health care issues in the United States speaks to the centrality of this issue to America's economy. Health care costs continue to rise rapidly in the United States and throughout the developed world, making this social problem even more economically vital to solve. Total U.S. health care expenditures are estimated to have grown from $2.39 trillion in 2008 to $2.50 trillion in 2009.[31] The health care market in the United States in 2009 comprised hospital care (about $789.4 billion), physician and clinical services ($539.1 billion), prescription drugs ($244.8 billion), nursing home and home health ($213.6 billion), dental care ($101.9 billion), and other items totaling $611.2 billion.[32]

Congress's 2010 passage of health care reform legislation will, if anything, only make this industry more attractive to business, given the government mandate that every American be insured. With forty-six million U.S. citizens uninsured when the legislation passed, there's a big business opportunity involved in solving this problem. It's also a matter of efficiency: 38 percent of Americans, both insured and uninsured, cite affordability of health care as the country's most significant health care problem.[33] These statistics point to problems but also potential: the private sector can both address social needs and also drive profits by innovating solutions and lowering costs.

Global Development

One clear nexus of business opportunity and social change is the increasing focus on the bottom of the pyramid (BOP). The BOP is the world's largest and poorest socioeconomic group: an estimated four billion people living on less than $2 per day, in the slums of Brazil and India, the villages of Africa, and many other places. At the same time, the BOP's purchasing power is an estimated $5 trillion.[34] And by the year 2050, 85 percent of consumers are expected to live in developing nations.[35] Companies are well aware of this: everyone from Starbucks to Sam's Club is setting their sights on these markets.

4. Philanthropy Has Become a Commodity

Philanthropy used to be a hallmark of distinction and social prestige for corporations and the well-heeled. Many corporations set up their own eponymous foundations in the 1960s and 1970s as a way of giving back to the community—and as a statement of success. Starting with the tremendous wealth creation in the 1980s, corporate foundations became more commonplace: between 1987 and 2007 the number of corporate foundations nearly doubled.[36] The total number of foundations grew at the same pace, more than doubling from 1992 to 2007.[37] But the bar for prestige ratcheted up even higher in 1997, when Ted Turner famously announced his $1 billion pledge to the United Nations, kicking off the age of mega-philanthropy. Since then, *Forbes* magazine has counted a total of thirteen more "billion dollar donors,"[38] from Bill Gates to Warren Buffett to Stephan Schmidheiny, the German industrialist. Big gifts have become so commonplace that when Virgin founder Richard Branson pledged $3 billion for environmental causes at the Clinton Global Initiative in 2006, it barely caused a stir. The pervasiveness of philanthropy has in some ways lessened its "wow value"; not only does philanthropy now add little distinction to a corporation's reputation, but it is simply expected of any successful corporation.

5. The Value of Intangible Assets Is Rising

I mentioned earlier that Bloomberg now carries ESG data for companies. Starting in late 2009, the financial service behemoth's terminals featured ESG for about three thousand companies. By some estimates, more than a third of a company's total value is now determined by such soft, or intangible, nonfinancial factors.[39] According to Jon Low, author of the book *Invisible Advantage*, intangible assets account for up to 50 percent of the market value of most large industrial and services companies.[40] Low argues that traditional assets and earnings have declined dramatically as predictors of stock performance in recent decades, as evidenced by the increasing value institutional investors and portfolio managers place on nonfinancial information—like social value created within and outside of the company.

And companies are aware of this, as suggested by their attempts to publicize ESG-related efforts: ExxonMobil, Microsoft, American Electric Power, and others routinely publish "Sustainability" and "Citizenship" reports; a 2009 Coca-Cola 10-K filing outlined water scarcity risks and how they are affected by climate change; and National Grid has disclosed how it's linking executive pay to greenhouse gas reduction targets.[41]

What the Social Capital Market Means for Business

There's no disputing that the social capital market is real and growing. The fundamental fact that the market now attaches economic value to social impact forces companies to rethink many things: marketing, recruiting, innovation, philanthropy, partnerships, and business models, to name a few. At the same time, there are some very practical implications of the SCM for corporate strategy. These fundamental principles lay the groundwork for this book and will inform the next generation of corporate social strategies.

- *It's not just about reputation anymore.* In an era of responsible business, touting the fact that you *are* responsible is no longer distinctive. Corporate philanthropy is more expected than heralded. As a result, the primary driver for corporate social strategy is no longer reputation—it's results. Investors, employees, and consumers in the SCM value real social impact and real business results.

- *It's okay to expect an economic return for doing good.* The advent of socially responsible investing, microlending, cause-related marketing, and sustainability strategies has made it socially acceptable to link the concepts of profit and social impact. It is no longer shameful for executives to require a business justification for social investments and strategies. This mind-set has only been reinforced by the acceptance of social entrepreneurship as a viable nonprofit strategy, the affirmative support of policymakers for an expanded corporate role in solving social problems, and the wave of new businesses focused on environmental sustainability.

- *Social strategies must become business strategies.* The tremendous value placed by the SCM on social and environmental impact requires that companies create new models for social engagement that are specifically designed to produce business results. Justifying traditional approaches like philanthropy, volunteering, and environmental compliance in business terms is not the same as creating real, tangible business value.

- *Measurement must become a core competency.* The SCM can't value what it can't measure. And the more capital—in terms of money, time, and effort—that pours into the SCM, the more people are asking, "Is this really making a difference—and if so, how much?" Management, consumers, investors, and others are holding corporate social responsibility (CSR) data to a higher level of scrutiny, studying data from financial statements, analyst reports, and other sources more carefully. It's no longer just about having reports, or metrics; it's about proving that meaningful social and business value is being created.

The SCM is challenging businesses to find new ways to create value. Think of the SCM as a huge "social arbitrage" opportunity for companies—indeed, social change may be the last great untapped business market. It is home to some of the largest profit pools today: insuring the uninsured, delivering alternative sources of energy, eliminating food deserts, alleviating poverty, and eradicating disease. Businesses that want to grow must find new ways to address these needs and to profit from doing so. This book explains how.

Chapter 2

RESPONSIBILITY IS NOT A STRATEGY

Reduce your carbon footprint.
Diversify your supply chain.
Give back to the community.
Pay a living wage.
Be accountable ... responsible.
... ethical.
... green.

Corporations just can't seem to win. Bullied for years by environmentalists, social activists, international watchdogs, and Michael Moore, companies have reluctantly embraced a responsibility agenda that is not their own. Put on the defensive, companies are doing what they can to keep pace: hiring eco-consultants, issuing sustainability reports, partnering with nonprofits, filling out media questionnaires, submitting to carbon audits, and attending compliance seminars, workshops, and conferences. The Gap has gone RED,[1] Avon has gone pink,[2] Coca-Cola has gone blue,[3] and just about everyone else is trying to go green.[4] In a near-frenzied state, companies are blindly whacking away at the piñata of social responsibility without even knowing what's inside. In private discussions, on conference panels, across the blogosphere, and throughout the published research, one thing is clear: companies are in a state of corporate social confusion. Why?

From Social Contract to Social Capital Market

The social capital market has fundamentally changed the role of business in society, making yesterday's corporate strategies obsolete. To stay relevant in this new economic reality, companies must rethink their corporate social playbooks. Why is this necessary? Because a new set of players—consumers, employees, Wall Street, suppliers, and business partners—are stepping into the Birkenstocks of social activists with a very different set of expectations. These new "stakeholders" are focused on positive social *and* business outcomes, not just compliance.

There's a lot at stake in getting this right. As stated in this book's introduction, companies spend a combined $32 billion annually on social responsibility efforts[5]; $11 billion on corporate giving alone.[6] The median amount of charitable giving alone for a Fortune 100 company is $50 million.[7] To put that in perspective, for the last several years oil companies like Exxon and Royal Dutch Shell have each been spending well over $100 million *annually* on corporate social responsibility (CSR) efforts.[8]

Historically, companies have viewed social involvement as a matter of ethics—a responsibility to "give back" and to be a "good corporate citizen." Under the old logic—a tacit agreement called the *social contract*—corporations were expected to support the local community and minimize the negative impact of their business, in return for the right to reap profits. To meet these obligations, companies developed social contract strategies such as grantmaking to local charities, volunteering, and compliance. In addition to charitable giving, companies have come under increasing pressure to curb certain behaviors deemed unethical or irresponsible. Think: pollution (the "green" movement), human rights (child labor in Nike's shoe factories), workers' rights (Walmart's low wages), health hazards (McDonald's Supersize fries), governance and accountability (everything about Enron), and negligent behavior (remember the Exxon Valdez?). Some religious groups and social activists have gone so far as to deem entire industries irresponsible (such as tobacco, alcohol, gambling, and defense, to name a few).

Over the last twenty years, society's expectations of companies have grown significantly. According to a recent survey of CEOs, 95 percent said that society now has higher expectations that business will shoulder public responsibilities than it did five years ago.[9] Thus companies have had to expand their *social contract* responsibilities—the more formalized responsibilities encompassed by CSR. CSR now embraces a wide range of disciplines: corporate governance and ethics programs; health, safety, and environment programs; attention to human and labor rights; human resource management policies; community involvement; respect for indigenous groups and minorities; corporate philanthropy and employee volunteering; adherence to principles of fair competition; anti-bribery and anti-corruption measures; accountability, transparency, and performance reporting; and responsible supplier relations.[10]

McDonald's actions provide a great illustration of a traditional corporate approach to CSR, demonstrating responsibility to community, environment, employees, and suppliers.[11] McDonald's has a dedicated CSR staff that focuses on a range of compliance activities, as well as an embedded staff in key areas that address sustainability, like packaging, energy, and construction. One example is supply chain management, such as ensuring that 91 percent of McDonald's fish is sourced from sustainable fisheries or that its beef suppliers recycle their tallow into diesel fuel.[12] Other responsibility efforts include supplier diversity, resource conservation, animal welfare, employee welfare, product safety, nutrition, and corporate governance. As for transparency, McDonald's issues its own annual *Worldwide Corporate Responsibility Report* that tracks compliance metrics such as "percent of nine largest markets that provide nutrition information out-of-restaurant (i.e., websites)" or "percent of suppliers who have affirmed McDonald's Code of Conduct."[13] The report is even presented online rather than in print form, to conserve paper and demonstrate commitment to the environment.

These strategies, which are similar to those of other firms, are focused on two primary functions: doing good (philanthropy) and not doing bad (compliance with responsible management practices). There may well be some incidental business benefits—such as cost savings, less risk, employee satisfaction, and positive press coverage—but that's really not the point. The point is to satisfy the *social contract*.

So why is everyone confused? Because in today's social capital market, the old social contract mind-set—where doing good was good enough—is no longer enough. To win in the social capital market, companies must transcend this way of thinking. Stakeholders in the social capital market have a much higher set of expectations for companies. To be sure, everyone expects companies to continue to meet their social contract obligations. But investors, CEOs, and Wall Street analysts are also looking for social strategies to produce short-term, tangible business value. And employees, consumers, nonprofits, and civic leaders are looking for companies to do more than minimize the fallout from their operations: they expect companies to proactively *solve* social problems.

Why Companies Can't Win

The problem isn't that companies are failing to be more responsible, ethical, sustainable, or any other such quality. Most are. The problem is that most social contract strategies are designed to reduce risk, not to produce business value. Let's take a closer look at the limitations of our current approach to social change.

1. Being Good Is Defined as "Not Being Bad"

After one of my recent speeches, an executive in the audience relayed a question his CEO always asks: "Why do we have to give back? We never took anything!" In the responsibility regime, companies are in a constant state of ethical deficit: they're presumed socially irresponsible until proven otherwise.

What's more, it's not exactly clear what social responsibility is. The metrics used by CSR evaluators are fairly subjective and thus difficult to manage against. A few years ago, the corporate citizenship director for a large consumer packaged goods company was asked to report to her CEO on the success of the company's social responsibility work. The director decided that inclusion in the Dow Jones Sustainability Index would be a reasonable proxy for the company's success at sustainability. So the director completed the Dow Jones Sustainability survey (administered by Sustainability Asset Management, a Swiss firm). The survey posed such questions as these:

- Does your company use a uniform group-wide risk analysis framework?

- Which of the following aspects are covered by your anti-corruption and bribery policy?

- What approaches does your company use for integrating customer feedback?

- Does your company publicly endorse the ILO Tripartite Declaration of Principles concerning Multinational Enterprises and Social Policy?

Upon completing the survey, the citizenship director was told that the firm ranked in the 50th percentile when compared to peer companies in the Index. The next year, the director completed the Dow Jones survey again, only this time she answered one question differently (relating to evaluating philanthropic grants). The company's rank soared to the 95th percentile! Bottom line: current ways of measuring social responsibility don't prove much. As one blogger noted when reviewing *Fortune*'s list of socially responsible companies, "Oil giants BP and Shell are No. 2 and No. 3, respectively, and four of the top ten on the list are utilities. That's because the rankings don't measure performance outcomes such as CO_2 emissions. Instead, they look at management practices: *Does a company have procedures for listening to critics? Are its executives and board members accountable? Has it hired an external verifier?*"[14]

As a result, companies are left to harmonize a cacophony of voluntary standards, norms, codes, and regulations with overlapping geographies, issues, and constituencies. Among the most notable: Australian Criminal Code Act, Caux Round Table Principles for Business, CERES Principles, EMAS, Ethical Trading Initiative, Forest Stewardship Council, Global Reporting Initiative, Global Sullivan Principles, Humane Cosmetics Standard, ICFTU Basic Code of Labour Practice, Investors in People, ICC Business Charter for Sustainable Development, ISO 14001, OHSAS18001, PERI Reporting Guidelines, Social Accountability 8000 (SA8000), South African Government Employment Equity Act, Sunshine Corporate Reporting, the U.S. Government Federal Sentencing Guidelines, and don't forget the FTSE4 Good Breast-Milk Substitute Criteria.[15] There are even rules for how to *report* on all these rules, such as the Accountability AA1000 standard requiring materiality, stakeholder inclusiveness, sustainability, completeness, reliability, clarity, balance, comparability, accuracy, and timeliness.[16]

Bottom line: in the social contract world, the best companies can do is to meet society's expectations for being a responsible business—and even that is tough!

2. Social Responsibility Is Now Just the Baseline for Doing Business

Today, almost all companies make charitable donations, encourage volunteering, offer recycling programs, support diversity, and talk up the importance of being a good corporate citizen. According to a recent KPMG study, more than half the world's largest companies issue stand-alone corporate responsibility reports, and 64 percent discuss responsibility in their annual financial reports.[17] Over 1,200 companies have issued a sustainability report, including Panasonic,

McDonald's, Nike, Procter & Gamble, Baxter, General Motors, and British Airways.[18] Companies are expected to take care of their employees, give to charity, and not pollute. Many companies boast of their compliance with human rights guidelines and other labor standards as evidence of their social responsibility. The result: no one really stands out anymore for being socially responsible—it just looks really bad when they're not.

Not getting credit for being responsible isn't such a bad thing: making responsibility integral to the way companies do business today is what the CSR movement is all about. Having gained acceptance inside most large corporations and on Wall Street, "being responsible" is now just par for the course. But the success of CSR has also created new challenges, particularly when it comes to building a business case. Many companies have justified their substantial investment in social contract strategies based on the belief that CSR will help distinguish the firm and enhance its brand reputation. But in a world where everyone is "socially responsible," being good has little reputational advantage.

3. Most Companies' Social Agendas Aren't Their Own

This past year, amidst the major economic downturn, I attended a corporate philanthropy conference focused on education. Dozens of Fortune 500 companies were there. At the end of the conference, a community affairs director from one of the Big Four auditing firms approached me and said, "This is such hard work, and we have failed. We haven't been able to figure out a solution to America's education problem." I started to offer some consolation, and then it struck me: *Wait a minute! Since when is it your job to fix education in America? Does your CEO know that this is what you're doing while your firm is fighting to stay alive?*

That example shows how far companies have gone in internalizing social agendas that were never theirs in the first place. In the past, companies have been influenced by a group of nontraditional stakeholders: international NGOs, academics, blogger-activists, consultants, and environmental experts. These include standard-setting bodies like the Global Reporting Initiative and the United Nations Global Compact. These organizations promulgate ethics and reporting guidelines for companies and have deeply influenced the way companies define social responsibility "success." Other influencers include thought leaders like Business for Social Responsibility Accountability and Ceres. These groups encourage companies to adopt sustainable business practices, provide technical assistance, convene conferences, and generally serve as promoters for the CSR movement. Companies are also influenced by published rankings and social responsibility indexes. These include research firms like KLD Analytics and Innovest (both recently acquired by Risk Metrics Group), as well as indexes like the Dow Jones Sustainability Index and FTSE 4 Good that track the financial performance of companies meeting various corporate responsibility standards.

This complex web of stakeholders complicates the agenda for companies. Absent their own proactive agenda, many companies have had their social profile defined by others, to the point that consumers associate them reflexively: Nike = child labor; McDonald's = obesity; Walmart = low wages; ExxonMobil = environmental damage; Philip Morris = cancer. As these examples suggest, social contract strategies have set up a rebuttable presumption for companies: that you are socially irresponsible until you prove otherwise. The influence of third parties over corporate social agendas is just another reason why the best companies can do on social responsibility is break even.

4. Social Contract Strategies Weren't Designed to Produce Business Value

Most companies pursuing social contract strategies today struggle with measuring their business value. Some hire outside consultants or "social auditors"; others try out new frameworks and "social return on investment" methodologies. Having advised companies for years on measuring CSR strategies, I have realized why measuring business impact is so challenging: social contract strategies were never designed to produce these types of outcomes. Strategies like philanthropy, volunteering, transparency, and compliance reporting were designed to satisfy the social contract, not to generate economic returns for the business. Giving employees a day off to do volunteer work, although it could increase employee engagement, has no measurable business value—it's just a nice thing to do. More studies and analysis won't change that fact. Indeed, after a careful review of the studies asserting a link between CSR and profitability, David Vogel, author of the book *The Market for Virtue*, concluded: "[T]here is no evidence that behaving more virtuously makes firms more profitable."[19]

A few years ago McDonald's was under heavy attack by Morgan Spurlock (whose *Super Size Me* film documentary, with Spurlock himself as the guinea pig, highlighted all the dangers of an all–Golden Arches diet) and Eric Schlosser (whose book *Fast Food Nation* pointed out the negative effects of McDonald's on consumers, global food suppliers, and small businesses). The media piled on. Customers began to feel guilty just walking through the door. McDonald's was having a major run on what the company calls their "trust bank." Being green, sourcing sustainable coffee, and requiring that hens each have a minimum of 72 square inches of space to move around in couldn't fix that. It barely even buffered it. McDonald's fixed its trust problem by *fixing its trust problem*: the company ditched the Supersize fries and drinks and introduced an array of healthy meal options including salads, yogurt parfaits, and apple dippers—McDonald's is now the world's largest buyer of apples. All of the socially responsible efforts the company has undertaken have done what they were designed to do: mitigate exposure to certain social and environmental risks. But as you would expect, the social strategies that have the biggest influence over business outcomes are those that affect the *core business*—in the case of McDonald's, adding healthy options to its menu.

Still, companies aspire to be more "strategic" with their philanthropy. For example, management thought leaders have long advocated that companies identify philanthropic causes and initiatives that are more closely "linked to their business" or competitive context.[20] According to one expert, "this approach would suggest American Express supporting a dance company because its business relates to entertainment."[21] But let's face it: no one is likely to apply for an American Express credit card *because* the company sponsored the ballet. It was just a nice philanthropic gesture. Although it's a step in the right direction, making philanthropy more strategic has inherent limitations because philanthropy itself was never designed to benefit the business. Certainly companies should aspire to satisfy the social contract in ways that make the most sense for the business. But as pressure from the social capital market mounts, companies are trying to stretch social contract strategies into business strategies, and that simply doesn't work.

A U.S. apparel company learned this lesson a few years ago. In the wake of closing its North American plants and sending its manufacturing overseas, the company focused its philanthropy on workers' rights initiatives, including training factory workers on asset-building strategies (basically, assisted savings plans). Under growing pressure from management to "align social impact with the business," the community affairs team tried to extend this strategy by making grants to nonprofits that could help the company's U.S. retail store workers "build assets" too by saving money for college, with the hope that this would boost retention. But the strategy made no sense: the average retail worker in America didn't need counseling about their rights or help saving $500—most were suburban kids working at shopping malls. Moreover, it was clear that asset building wasn't going to have any impact on employee turnover in the stores—the primary business challenge. The bottom line: social contract strategies aren't business strategies, and they are not designed to generate business value.

5. Social Contract Strategies Weren't Designed to Solve Social Problems

Perhaps the greatest irony in this arena is that social contract strategies also have limited social value. Most of today's corporate strategies aren't really designed to solve a particular social problem—even many of the best "green" corporate strategies heralded by media commentators and sustainability advocates aren't actually designed to *improve* the environment; they're primarily designed to damage it less. Moreover, most of the charitable donations that companies make are quite small—in 2007, the average grant for a company with a total philanthropy budget under $5 million was $23,200, and for companies who give over $100 million, the average grant was only $61,900.[22] It's hard to make a real difference with intravenous drip–style funding.

Even social strategies that are designed to have social impact sometimes don't. Ben & Jerry's, one of the corporate grandfathers of social responsibility, found this out the hard way when the company tried to help out the Amazon rainforest in the late 1980s. Ben Cohen, one of the company's founders, thought he'd found the perfect solution: sourcing Brazilian nuts directly from the Amazon rainforest for the company's then-new flavor Rainforest Crunch. The carton label read: "money from these nuts will help Brazilian forest peoples start a nut-shelling cooperative."[23] The strategy was intended to provide indigenous people with alternative career options to mining and clear-cutting, so it was good for them and the environment. As it turned out, the Xapuri co-op—the Brazilian cooperative expected to produce the nuts—couldn't deliver the quantity or quality needed, and ultimately went out of business. Ben & Jerry's purchased more than a million pounds of nuts, and the cooperative processed only fifty thousand pounds that met U.S. standards.[24] Rainforest Crunch was discontinued several years later.

Ben & Jerry's had its heart in the right place, but as is true of many well-intentioned strategies, when the benefit to the business is incidental, so too is the impact on society. By failing to design a careful, comprehensive strategy to drive both sustainable business and social value, Ben & Jerry's failed to deliver either. When the primary intent of a strategy is philanthropic, companies are inherently limited in the resources they can commit and often cannot throw the full weight of the business behind a particular social problem. As a result, companies resort to piecemeal efforts like grants and scholarships, rather than systemic solutions to social problems.

We Need a New Approach

If being good simply means not being bad, we have set the bar too low. Requiring that companies mitigate the fallout from their own harmful activities merely breaks even in the social impact calculus. The social contract era can be credited with opening the eyes of corporate America to the importance of social and environmental issues, and of motivating corporations to conform their activities to a heightened set of standards. That's no small feat. But now it's time to elevate the game and offer companies a new way forward that directly links positive social change to increased business value.

To link social change and business outcomes, companies must rethink their approach to social change. This isn't a matter of retrofitting your existing social contract strategies with better business justifications; it's about coming up with fresh, innovative strategies that are *specifically designed* to create business value through social change.

What are these new social strategies? That's where social innovation, the subject of the next chapter, comes in.

Chapter 3

CORPORATE SOCIAL INNOVATION

Maybe the most important way that we at Walmart believe in giving back is through our commitment to using the power of this enormous enterprise as a force for change.[1]

—Sam Walton, founder of Walmart

Levi Strauss and Co. had a problem. In the early 1960s, as the iconic U.S. apparel-maker prepared to open its first southern U.S. manufacturing plant in Blackstone, Virginia, the city's civic leaders demanded that the company hire only white workers. But Levi's refused, threatening to move its factory to another city if it couldn't be integrated. Eyeing local jobs, the civic leaders agreed to allow blacks in the same facility—so long as they were separated from whites at all times. Levi's stood its ground. Eventually the city backed off, and Levi's opened one of the first integrated workplaces in Virginia.[2]

This move, which predated the Civil Rights Act of 1964 and other federally mandated desegregation laws, exemplifies social innovation—how companies can use the *machinery* of the business to create positive social change. Indeed, business has always been at the forefront of innovating solutions to social problems—it was just never thought of as a business strategy. In this example, Levi's was clearly focused on promoting positive social change by forcing desegregation; but it was unclear whether they were considering the potential business value (such as a more productive workforce and a new customer base). Today, companies across sectors—from GE to Coca-Cola to Travelers Insurance—are beginning to recognize the power of social change as a strategy for fueling business growth.

The preceding chapters set up a challenge for corporate strategists: if social issues are now business issues, how do we transform social strategies into business strategies? The answer, as those chapters suggest, is *not* more charity, compliance, or social responsibility. The answer is *social innovation*. This chapter defines what social innovation is and how it works.

Defining Social Innovation

We live in an era of corporate social *everything*. Companies have created just about every possible combination of business and social impact—corporate social responsibility, corporate sustainability, corporate social entrepreneurship, corporate social intrapreneurship, corporate social investing, corporate community involvement, creative capitalism, strategic philanthropy, philanthrocapitalism, cause-related marketing, cause branding, and on and on—in an effort to crack the code of the social capital market. But getting to the right answer requires asking the right questions. For those operating in the social capital market, the right question is clear: *How do you generate* business value *through solving social problems?*

As detailed in the preceding chapter, many business leaders are still operating in a social contract paradigm, trying to retrofit business justifications to philanthropy and compliance strategies. I've spent years measuring the business impact of corporate philanthropy and social responsibility efforts, coming to understand a simple truth: most of these strategies have no impact on the bottom line. To produce the results that businesses desire, we need a new generation of strategies—strategies that are *specifically designed to generate economic value through positive social change*. That's what social innovation is about.

Before diving more deeply into what social innovation is, let's clarify what it isn't.

What Social Innovation Is Not

Social innovation is not corporate social responsibility. Most corporate responsibility efforts to date are rooted in the theory that creating social value is an obligation for companies to "give back" and be "good corporate citizens," as part of their social contract. To satisfy this obligation, companies have developed a variety of strategies including grant-making, employee volunteering, and even the recent sustainability or "green" initiatives. Each is aimed at supporting important social causes or minimizing the negative effects of businesses (for example, on the environment); as a result, such efforts generally fall into the categories of philanthropy (doing good) or compliance (not doing bad).

Many expect that philanthropy and compliance will lead to business benefits, such as improved reputation, customer loyalty, and employee retention. But the research has been inconclusive, largely because these efforts are often too diffuse (grants to the community) or insubstantial (volunteer days) to produce any measurable impact on the bottom line. In most cases, business justifications are made after the fact, as a secondary rationale for philanthropic strategies. If in fact the primary intention was to benefit the business, there are probably more direct and cost-effective strategies a company could pursue, such as well-designed PR campaigns or new compensation and benefits programs.

That's not to say that corporate social responsibility and other philanthropic efforts are not valuable—they can and do generate real benefits to employees, nonprofits, and communities. But social innovation offers companies an even more powerful approach.

That's because social innovation is focused primarily on driving business value—leveraging the *machinery of the business* to solve social problems. The business impact is tangible, direct, and near-term. And social innovation offers more meaningful and lasting social change because it is predicated on actual solutions to social and environmental problems; anything less wouldn't create enough value to be economically significant.

Social innovation is not strategic philanthropy. In the preceding chapter I described how some companies have tried to stretch social contract strategies into business strategies, through "strategic philanthropy" and other means. These strategies are a form of philanthropy, characterized by a defined focus or theme, which may or may not be associated with a company's strategy. Most strategic philanthropy initiatives focus on social or environmental issues that are tangential to the business: improving local schools, encouraging kids to lead healthy lifestyles, preserving natural resources, increasing technology literacy for adults, and the like. Although these efforts may ultimately improve the environment in which a company operates (or its "competitive context"), their impact and time frame are too far removed from near-term business priorities. Moreover, there is a real limit to how far companies can "stretch" philanthropy to produce any tangible, direct business value (particularly when given through corporate foundations, which are limited by IRS private inurement rules).

In general, strategic philanthropy is a charity-focused tactic aimed at creating a strategic intersection with the business, whereas social innovation is a business strategy that creates a positive intersection with society. Social innovation is transparent in its intent to benefit the business *directly*.

Social innovation is not values-driven business. There are many "good" companies out there today that are ethical and philanthropic, transparent and accountable, that treat their employees with respect, recycle, use compostable packaging and cutlery, and show genuine commitment to the double bottom line of doing well by doing good or even the triple bottom line of business, community, and environment. These companies are case-studied, analyzed, and held up as high-purpose, values-driven, sustainable vanguards—firms that put values first and profits second. Because of these characteristics, these companies are more likely to benefit from higher employee satisfaction, lower turnover, greater openness to innovation, more loyal customers, and strong relationships with governments and nonprofits. Professor James Austen of Harvard Business School calls these firms "corporate social entrepreneurs" whose very purpose "migrates from one of maximizing returns to investors to optimizing returns to stakeholders ... who are significantly affected by company actions and who can in turn impact the company."[3]

Timberland is regarded as a corporate social entrepreneur. Says CEO Jeff Swartz: "We operate on the core theory, on the belief that doing well and doing good ... are inextricably linked and that everything we do, every business decision we make, every strategy we promulgate, every speech we make, or every pair of boots or shoes that we ship, have to be the embodiment of commerce and justice, and that's a different model."[4] Indeed, it is a very different model from business as usual, but it is not social innovation. Social innovation is not about putting profits second, or doing good and hoping that it adds up to something beneficial for the business. It is a more direct linkage, forged by intentionally putting positive social change in the way of the business. Although most social innovators are of course values-driven, they view social and environmental impact first and foremost as components of business strategy, not merely as ethical standards.

Some, like Bill Gates, have pushed the idea of "values-driven" business closer to social innovation. It's what Mr. Gates calls "creative capitalism"—an effort to combine the pursuit of profits with the desire to serve the needs of those who may lack the means to pay for new technologies. For example, Microsoft, in addition to its philanthropy, is working on projects like a visual interface that will enable illiterate or semiliterate people to use a PC instantly, with minimal training. Another project involves developing new software that allows a classroom full of students to use one computer at the same time.[5] Although such strategies focus better on using the core business than many, they're still philanthropic in nature—using profits from the core business to donate or subsidize technologies for poorer markets. Social innovation, on the other hand, is about innovating creative, market-based solutions to social problems that result in high-growth, profitable business opportunities.

So What Is Social Innovation?

Let's start with a few examples.

• *Coca-Cola Recycling LLC.* In 2006, Coca-Cola Enterprises launched a for-profit subsidiary to capture, recycle, and reuse 100 percent of its beverage packaging in the United States. The company is investing more than $60 million to build the world's largest recycling plants. The strategy has huge implications for the business: making new aluminum cans from used cans takes 95 percent less energy, and twenty recycled cans can be made with the energy needed to produce one can using virgin ore.[6]

Social Innovation: Through the recycling effort, Coca-Cola is saving significant energy costs (business value) and reducing use of nonrenewable resources like energy and aluminum (social value).

• *Cummins in Africa.* Cummins Inc. is an engine manufacturer and technology company based in Columbus, Indiana. One of the fastest-growing segments of their business is power generation, particularly in parts of the world that lack fluent electricity. Sales gains in Africa, where Cummins sells thousands of diesel generators, were up 34 percent in 2009, more than in any other region of the world.[7] But Cummins' business growth in Africa is being threatened by a shortage of skilled technicians who can maintain their generators. So Cummins devised a business strategy to partner with technical institutes, like the Ithemba Institute of Technology in South Africa, to train African youth on how to work with and repair Cummins diesel engines. Students get jobs, and Cummins gets a talent pipeline that will support its business growth throughout the region.[8]

Social Innovation: Cummins is using the training partnerships to gain much-needed talent (business value) while providing work opportunities for underserved African youth (social value).

- *Tesco.* Tesco, the world's third-largest food retailer, is opening small outlets offering healthier ready-to-eat meals and fresh produce in U.S. "food deserts"—areas currently underserved by grocery store chains.[9] As part of its initial strategy, the company aims to open over one hundred new stores in these areas in California, Nevada, and Arizona. Local communities have expressed excitement about having a wider range of food options than those provided by typical convenience stores, and Tesco gains entry into a potentially lucrative new market (it's the company's first entry into the United States) with the strategy—one in which Tesco's familiarity with smaller-scale stores may give it an advantage over larger-format stores like major supermarkets and Walmart. Research on those shopping at the new-format Tesco stores showed significant improvement in their dietary habits.[10]

Social Innovation: Tesco's new outlets allow it to enter an important new market (business value) by bringing healthier food options to communities that need them desperately (social value).

Each of these examples illustrates the characteristics of social innovation. For Coca-Cola, Cummins, and Tesco, these were business strategies that leveraged social change as a way to drive profitable business growth. Each company used innovation to create real value from unrealized potential—whether a new market, discarded waste, or unemployed youth. Thus social innovation inverts the way that business sees social change, turning what was once a charitable proposition into a business opportunity.

Social innovations involve four key elements:

- *Intentional Business Strategy:* Social innovations are designed to solve a discrete business problem or accomplish a key business objective by pulling the levers of social change. They contribute directly to the bottom line by increasing revenues, penetrating markets, acquiring and retaining customers, developing talent, or containing costs. A key point: social innovation should hold up to the same level of business scrutiny and return-on-investment expectations as any other corporate strategy.

- *Leveraging the Core Business:* Social innovations use the "engine" of the business itself—the primary profit-making functions—to create economic value through social change. Social innovation initiatives are executed directly through the functional business units (such as marketing, sales, operations, R&D, HR).

- *Creating New Value:* Social innovations use innovation to unlock the potential of undervalued markets, customer segments, talent, and relationships. Social innovations leverage different aspects of the business—products, training, marketing, and R&D, to name a few—to create both social and business value.

- *Positive Social Change:* Social innovations achieve much more than charity or compliance—they affirmatively solve social problems by using the core business to increase access to products or services, lower costs, create economic opportunities for the underserved, or achieve public policy objectives. The social change is lasting and scalable because it is directly aligned with the incentives of the business.

The real "Aha!" behind social innovation is what I refer to as *social arbitrage*: discovering the hidden or unrealized business potential in social change. It's about creating new forms of value, derived primarily from achieving socially desirable outcomes. Social innovation finds ways to create profitable business opportunities from intractable social issues: education, health care, global development, hunger, even hand washing, to name a few. In the social capital market, there are new forms of value attached to social and environmental impact—some by investors, some by consumers, some by employees, some by government. The market will pay for things that these groups value. Corporations can also help the market learn to value new business and economic dimensions including underserved segments (such as the bottom of the pyramid), smaller scales (such as micro-sized personal care products for emerging markets), and different models (such as manual distribution networks). At the same time, this is not to assert that companies will save the world, or that all companies are good, or that the private sector should be setting social priorities. It's simply to say that we need to ask more from companies—we need to set the bar higher.

How Social Innovation Creates Value

There are countless different ways companies can tap into the value of the social capital market. Most approaches abide by a set of common principles for creating value. Some social innovations create value by *changing behavior*. It's hard to believe, but not long ago most of us weren't willing to pay a premium—or anything at all, really—for "green" or sustainable products. Now we routinely open our wallets for organic TV dinners, fair-trade coffee beans, and sustainable dog food. Why? Because marketers taught the market to value behaviors that are good for us and/or the environment—and now we're willing to pay for it. In the short term this kind of value creation can be profitable, and it has been. But if we want to stimulate longer-term market change and even greater profits, we need to find a way to make organic cheaper than conventional, or at least on par—just like we've made hybrid cars as fast as or even faster than gas-engine autos. That will cement behavioral changes in the market. Remember, humans are subject to the principles of behavioral economics, which means that as consumers we often act without rationality or logic. In this context, shifting market behavior toward options that create good social value—such as offering healthy food to individuals in food deserts—takes a lot of dedication and a little creativity.

Rather than changing behavior, some social innovations create value by *reducing costs*. Take for example innovations that lower costs. A simple illustration is GE's *ecomagination* line of products, many of which are industrial offerings with significant environmental benefits. Though the products involve significant short-term costs (certainly a higher cost than not buying them in the first place), because they decrease customers' long-term costs, they're willing to pay a premium for them. For example, GE offers a "Waste-to-Value" technology solution that allows customers (such as breweries) to reuse 99 percent of the wastewater they generate, saving millions of gallons of water annually (social value) while driving significant energy-cost savings (business value) by creating electricity and other energy from the wastewater.[11] So GE, their customers, and the environment benefit.

Another area in which social innovations can create value by reduction is scale. Microlending—the practice of allowing entrepreneurs (typically in developing countries) to borrow small amounts of money to start sustainable businesses—has led to dramatic profitability and positive social change. Now "microfying" has become an almost standard practice: more companies are using their existing infrastructure, knowledge, and technology to arbitrage markets and customer segments that were deemed previously unprofitable or undesirable, with reduced-scale offerings like microfranchising, micro-insurance, and many others.

Finally, social innovation creates value through *synergies*. One of the best examples is public-private partnerships (PPPs) in which corporations work directly with the government to achieve development goals—and business growth. A simple example is a partnership to develop infrastructure such as tollways or bridges. The company, the government, and the public all benefit. But today's PPPs—and potential ones—extend well beyond these established areas. Health insurance and vocational training are areas representing strong synergies between government and corporations. Companies can apply their technology and expertise to solve social problems profitably and without investing all their own resources, because the government or others share stakes in the same outcomes and will devote their resources to achieving these, as well. In a sense, one plus one equals three.

Why Social Innovation Makes Sense for Companies

Social innovation makes sense for companies and the global community, because it creates actual solutions to social problems (rather than temporary fixes or subsidies) and does so in a way that is sustainable, because it's actually profitable in a measurable way. Here are the primary reasons why it makes sense for most corporations to make social innovation a priority.

1. *Social innovation focuses on long-term value.* Unlike most philanthropic or other typical social responsibility efforts, social innovation uses the machinery of the business to drive profits within a market, segment, or set of offerings that make sense to target. Thus it forms a platform for real, sustainable profits.

2. *Social innovation relies on the core business versus ancillary resources and motivations.* The strategy is motivated first and

foremost by business goals, not *social contract* objectives. In this way it allows companies to devote substantially greater resources to social change. As Adam Smith said long ago: "It is not from the benevolence of the butcher, the brewer, or the baker, that we expect our dinner, but from their regard to their own interest."[12]

3. *Social innovation builds innovation skills, a core competency.* Getting executives and managers to think about how to use social change as a vehicle for profits—within the context of the core business—builds key competencies that can be used in driving more traditional organic growth.

4. *Social innovation is easy to measure.* Unlike most responsibility efforts, social innovation impacts the business in ways that are easy to measure because the strategies are tied directly to *business value.* So a given social innovation effort should drive revenues, profits, customer acquisition and retention, or any other metric by which any business initiative is measured. That allows companies to see easily which innovations make the cut—and by how much.

5. *Social innovation gives companies the opportunity for greater social impact.* By harnessing the full resources of the business— the engine, not the fumes—companies have the potential to create social impact that is more direct, lasting, and profound. And most importantly, social innovation creates the incentives for business to want to do more.

6. *Social innovation is both intentional and transparent.* Social innovation does not pretend to be "doing good" purely for the sake of doing good; it is an intentional business strategy. With transparency about this intent, companies no longer need to apologize for benefiting from the positive social outcomes they help produce. Clearly linking business goals to positive social results also liberates companies from any suspicion about ulterior motives.

If social innovation makes so much sense, why isn't everyone doing it? To be sure, some are. But many companies today are stuck in a paradigm in which responsibility and business are effectively mutually exclusive. Philanthropy is philanthropy and business is business. Businesses have attempted to create artificial overlap between the two—this is where the concepts of "strategic philanthropy" and more "socially responsible business" come in—but they haven't found the way to truly merge them. I remember when I first came to Chicago and wanted to start a socially responsible bank. I met with some investors, one of whom seemed quite intrigued (read: confused). He said, "So you're a charity?" No, it's a business, a commercial bank. "Oh, so then you have to give all of your profits away to charity, right?" No, it's a business, a commercial bank. No matter how many times or ways I tried to explain my idea, he just couldn't "get" the fact that this was simply a for-profit bank with a socially responsible mission (that is, focused on lending to nonprofits, women, and minority-owned businesses). As we left the meeting (I was empty-walleted, of course), he said, "Well, you know, I'm socially responsible. I don't beat my wife and I don't drink and drive!" And that was precisely the problem: this investor was stuck in a bifurcated world. Many companies still are too.

Others have called for a strategy like this before. Pfizer pretty much summed up social innovation in a recent business presentation when the company talked about its new emerging markets strategy as "meeting the diverse medical needs of patients in Emerging Markets around the world in an *innovative, socially responsible* and *commercially viable* manner." Similarly, during his 2007 Harvard commencement address, Bill Gates, now the world's largest philanthropist, called on the graduates to invent "a more creative capitalism" whereby "we can stretch the reach of market forces so that more people can make a profit, or at least make a living, serving people who are suffering from the worst inequities."[13] And in a December 2006 *Harvard Business Review* article, Harvard professor Clayton Christensen and coauthors suggest that because most social investments "are used to maintain the status quo," donors should invest their philanthropic funds in nonprofits and companies creating "catalytic innovations"—that is, low-cost services aimed at underserved segments.[14]

The increasing chorus of voices calling for social innovation reflects its urgency. But the challenge has been not so much whether the time is right for social innovation but *how* it can be done. In the past some great examples have been offered, and some good theories, but there just hasn't been a definitive methodology or roadmap that companies can use to develop social innovations of their own. That's what this book offers.

With this in mind, let's look at the fast-growing green movement and how it has set the stage for deeper social innovation.

Green: The First Color of a Rainbow of Social Innovations

The sustainability revolution can be considered the first major social innovation. But before sustainability became a business term, it was primarily a social activist's call to action.[15] So how did green break through?

Environmental advocates used a number of key strategies to take the movement from fringe to mainstream. But central to this process was making the principles of green more understandable to the business world and at the same time quantifying the real economic payoffs. One of the first steps was to change the language. Environmental advocates moved from the politics of "limits," "critiques," and "caps" to the politics of "possibility," "opportunity," and "potential."[16] As the movement gained speed, its terms and topics of choice became more fully business-oriented: the *costs* of failing to use environmentally friendly supplies, the power of making green part of your *brand*, the *customer segments* you could attract with greener products, and the *economic savings* you could reap from more environmentally efficient practices.

This shift helped to get big corporations on board—in part because they were taking more flak from an increasingly environmentally aware public, but largely because they saw the business value. Let's look at how this worked for Walmart. Despite huge revenues, in the middle of the first decade of the twenty-first century the retail giant faced ongoing reputation issues, with concerns surrounding its labor policies and competitive practices. According to a *Fortune* article, "The company's environmental record was nothing to boast about, either."[17] In fact, up to 8 percent of consumers had stopped shopping at Walmart because of such issues, according to a 2005 study.[18] So the costs of failing to focus on environmental issues—which could total well into the millions, given Walmart's volume—were becoming very clear.

Walmart acted quickly. In late 2005 CEO H. Lee Scott Jr. announced plans to reduce the corporation's environmental footprint, as part of a broad sustainability strategy built on three pillars: creating zero waste, using only renewable energy, and selling products that helped conserve resources and sustain the environment.[19] Scott didn't just send out a memo—he discussed the plan in a speech to all 1.6 million employees and about sixty thousand suppliers.

Of course Walmart wasn't doing this purely out of altruism—few companies do. Executives had come to realize that a much larger focus on the environment would help Walmart differentiate itself *and* push costs even lower through a more efficient supply chain and other means. So making Walmart's blue-and-white logo more green would drive greater business value through lower costs, sale of appealing environmentally focused products, and other sources—all while presenting a more acceptable public face. Walmart made good on its sustainability pledge by gathering external stakeholders who helped green their practices in key areas including seafood certification, an expanded organic cotton business (through partnership with nonprofits and government agencies), and more efficient, eco-friendly electronics; the company has also established a network of suppliers and other stakeholders that helps them find profitable routes to addressing a range of environmental issues.[20]

Walmart's focus on sustainability demonstrates how major corporations have broken through a barrier in their handling of environmental issues, transforming them from sources of complaints and charges to pathways to profitability. In fact, forward-thinking environment experts Michael Shellenberger and Ted Nordhaus chose to name their book *Break Through* and their organization the Breakthrough Institute, to signify the idea that environmentalism, as practiced now, has to die, "so that something new can be born."[21] As they suggested, that "something new" is a movement away from constraining human power and toward unleashing it, through an approach built on "expansive, pragmatic and holistic solutions." As an example, the authors point to Healthcare for Hybrids, a piece of legislation they helped then-Senator Obama develop four years ago: the bill would create a voluntary program whereby automakers could elect to receive federal financial assistance towards their retiree health care costs; in return, they'd be required to invest the savings in fuel-efficient-vehicle developments. Thus the program would help carmakers curb health care costs while reducing U.S. dependence on oil.

Across industries, examples of green innovation aren't hard to find. Dow Chemical has stepped up R&D in products including solar-power roof tiles and water-treatment technology for regions with clean-water shortages; according to Dow CEO Andrew Liveris, "There is 100 percent overlap between our business drivers and social and environmental interests."[22] Furniture company Herman Miller used a sustainability-focused approach that drove an 80-percent reduction in landfill waste and an 87-percent reduction in emissions and reportedly gained a 32-percent annual rate of return on these and related investments.[23] Bank of America's Manhattan skyscraper was designed to generate about 70 percent of its own energy; that made it more expensive than traditional buildings, but the company is expected to make money from the "green tower" through avenues including a lower operating cost, higher rent, and reductions in absenteeism.[24]

These are great examples of how the sustainability movement represents social innovation: its promoters created value by transforming an externality (a literal one in this case: the environment) from a liability (wherein the best a business can do is break even) into a clear business opportunity. Today, cost savings and market opportunities go hand in hand with the green movement. That's what Unilever CEO Patrick Cescau said about focusing on sustainability: "In the future it will be the only way to do business."[25] He said that two years ago, and the future is here. Green is a good start. But companies have to learn how to incorporate all the colors of the social innovation rainbow more broadly into their strategies and cultures.

Five Social Innovation Strategies

The five strategies here, detailed extensively in Part Two of this book, may not be the only routes to social innovation. But they are the synthesis of my years of measuring what companies are doing to drive business and social value simultaneously, whether they're doing this intentionally or not.

- *Create revenues through submarket products and services.* By working for markets previously considered impossible to address profitably, including the vast pool of uninsured U.S. citizens, food deserts of inner cities, and the millions of underserved at the bottom of the economic pyramid, companies reach new markets and consumers with a single strategy. Companies are making inroads into these large, untapped markets by microfying products and services, using trickle-up innovation, and applying other strategies.

- *Enter new markets through backdoor channels.* Today's biggest barriers to entering new markets are often not political or cultural, but social, including lack of talent, poverty, marginalized women, and so on. So corporations are building local talent (such as village women as sales reps) and partnering with governments and NGOs to enter these markets—in which they create real social value and profits. In this way, companies using backdoor market entry are finding innovative channels through which to enter new, often overlooked, and profitable markets.

- *Build emotional bonds with customers.* This is the future of brand marketing, as companies are building a deeper sense of purpose for their brands, customers' experience, and the company as a whole by engaging social problems. Whether raising the visibility of important social issues like teacher-funded classrooms or providing direct social benefits to their own consumers, companies are empowering customers to become part of the solution, and in doing so they are deepening loyalty, creating new customers, and turning consumers into brand ambassadors, which ultimately increases the bottom line.

- *Develop new pipelines for talent.* Public education and other systems aren't fostering the skills corporations need most, so businesses are creating talent-development pipelines that promote these capabilities while opening up new career opportunities for community members. These pipelines take the form of industry-sponsored training academies, apprenticeships, and specially designed curricula.

- *Influence policy through reverse lobbying.* Rather than lobbying hard for reduced regulations or other industry benefits, corporations are working with the public sector to reduce risk and generate business value—while solving social problems. This means lobbying for legislation that's good for business and society, offering goods and services through public-private partnerships, and other strategies.

In the next part of the book we'll explore these strategies further and offer tips, rich examples, and lessons learned from implementing them.

Part II

FIVE STRATEGIES FOR CORPORATE SOCIAL INNOVATION

Now that social change has become a critical driver of business growth, companies must figure out how to convert their "do good" *philanthropic* strategies into social impact *business* strategies. As suggested in Chapter Three, environmental sustainability is the closest we've come so far. Even so, most corporate "green" strategies aren't exactly making the world any better—they're just making it a little "less worse." We can do better. The next five chapters reveal the leading social innovation strategies that all companies can use to grow their business by solving important social problems.

I didn't set out to find these strategies; they sort of found me. My focus for the past sixteen years has been on measuring social impact—helping companies, nonprofits, and governments measure the performance of their CSR strategies, programs, and policies. What I found in working with companies surprised me: most social strategies had no measurable business value. Why? Because they were never designed to create business value in the first place. When old-time business leaders say that philanthropy and social responsibility are "just the right thing to do," they're speaking from a social contract mind-set. But the social capital market liberates companies from this unilaterally altruistic mind-set. Today, with the right strategies, companies don't have to be ashamed about reaping economic benefits from investing in social change. In fact, it's encouraged. Customers want to do business with a company whose values they share; employees want to work at a firm that stands for something. So social change has become an important part of business strategy. We've changed our expectations; now we need to change our strategy.

Chapter 4

STRATEGY ONE: CREATE REVENUES THROUGH SUBMARKET PRODUCTS AND SERVICES

Krisztina Holly, executive director of the University of Southern California's Stevens Institute for Innovation, once said that innovation involves a combination of products and processes that allow the successful translation of "new ideas into tangible societal impact."[1] She wasn't even talking about social innovation, just plain innovation. But embedded in the concept of innovation is the idea that products have the power to change the way we live and interact in society. Think about innovations like Facebook or the iPod. Now imagine what the world could be like if there were actually a financial incentive to harness that tremendous creativity and business ingenuity and apply it to solving social problems. That's the social innovation of submarket products and services. This chapter describes the trends behind this strategy, and how companies are using submarket products and services to expand market share, enter new markets, and reach greater economies of scale.

Tonik: Health Insurance for the Young Invincibles

One of the most promising U.S. health care innovations emerged from one of the least likely demographics: the "young invincibles," adults between nineteen and twenty-nine, Gen Y-ers who also happen to make up the largest percentage of uninsured people in America—close to one third!

As the segment's name implies, it's easy to imagine that this group tends not to buy health insurance because they believe they don't need it. Mounting evidence suggests that's wrong: the biggest reason young adults are uninsured is not because they feel invincible, but because they simply cannot afford it. It's the result of a double whammy. First, when people turn nineteen, most can no longer be covered by their parents' health care plans, but they're not yet eligible for Medicaid coverage; thus many young adults fall through the cracks in the insurance market.[2] Second, according to a report by the CommonWealth Fund, two-thirds of young adults don't have health insurance because of high costs.[3] So although many may want to be covered by the health insurance system that turns its back on them in their last year as teens, most can't afford to be.

It's a big problem. According to the latest U.S. Census data, in 2007 there were an estimated 13.2 million uninsured young adults, or about one out of every three. Adults younger than thirty-five are nearly twice as likely to be uninsured as adults forty-five and older. And young adults are also the fastest-growing group of uninsured Americans today. Any way you look at it, it's a population that is significantly underserved by the market. And that market failure, neglect, or misunderstanding is costing young people (and eventually, taxpayers) dearly.

WellPoint, the nation's largest health insurer, was well aware of the challenges faced by the uninsured, especially the young invincibles. But instead of viewing this social problem through the lens of their foundation, WellPoint saw it as a business opportunity through the lens of innovation. Several factors led them to take action: (1) it became clear that the high rate of uninsured people would eventually be addressed by the government if the industry didn't do something about it; (2) uninsured young adults represented a major untapped market—about 1.6 million in California alone; (3) expanding the overall market for health insurance was a better way to grow than constantly "trading" the same customers back and forth with competitors.[4]

WellPoint needed a scalable solution. The company decided to develop a low-cost but profitable health care insurance product aimed at uninsured young adults. What they came up with was Tonik, a meticulously researched, carefully planned, and brilliantly marketed new insurance offering. In a unique approach to product development, WellPoint used a "reverse point-of-view" analysis to carefully examine the preferences and lifestyles of uninsured young adults.[5] For example, rather than assuming that this segment lacked a fundamental interest in health insurance, as many competitors might have, WellPoint took the time to research the young invincibles, finding out they didn't see themselves as so invincible after all: specifically, they were interested in health insurance, *if* it met their needs and was offered at the right price. "We became convinced that the 'young invincibles' were willing and ready to take responsibility for their own health care—if they found a plan that fit their needs," said Mary Floyd, vice president of Sales Individual Business for Anthem Blue Cross, a WellPoint affiliate.[6]

WellPoint's research helped the company design a product addressing the new target segment's needs. First offered in 2004 in California, Tonik plan premiums can cost as little as little $79 to $211 per month for a twenty-five-year-old male; the policy covers major and routine medical care, prescriptions, dental and vision care, and even preventive care and emergency room visits. Tonik offers three plans attuned to distinct young adult lifestyles, as the names suggest: the Thrill-Seeker plan, the Part-Time Daredevil plan, and the Calculated Risk-Taker plan. Each plan differs by deductible, monthly premium, and number of doctor visits covered, depending on the package the customer selects.

Tonik used a hip campaign (example: "Say What's Up to Tonik") to appeal to young invincibles, but first and foremost Tonik was just smart business. Specifically, the strategy offers WellPoint a large and profitable new demographic and a point of entry into other specialty markets. Consumers are snapping up the novel policies that WellPoint markets. Sold on sites like Tonikhealth.com and Soundhealth.com, they're a hit with those aged nineteen to twenty-nine, and a big part of the way WellPoint has sold coverage to some 780,000 previously uninsured people in the last two years, says WellPoint's CEO Angela Braly.[7] Although that's just a fraction of the nation's 46 million uninsured—and of the 34.1 million that WellPoint covers—the effort has been "incredibly successful," the CEO says.[8]

Tonik has already had significant social impact. With the introduction of Tonik, WellPoint has been able to convince young invincibles to get covered: of the initial Tonik applicants in California, 70 percent were previously uninsured.[9]

At a time when its competitors were using foundations to provide "charity coverage" and support causes ranging from obesity prevention to Martin Luther King day, WellPoint executives realized that they could make even greater—and more lasting—social impact if they leveraged their core business. "Ever notice how big ideas seem inevitable after the fact?" WellPoint's website asks. Their success with Tonik certainly illustrates this notion.

The *Innovation*: Why This Strategy Works

Ultra-low-cost products are certainly not new. The Family Dollar Store has been around since 1959. Wendy's launched its $1 menu in 1989. Tata Motors introduced the Nano, the world's least expensive automobile, in 2008. But what is new is the idea that companies can leverage commercial products and services to solve social problems—not as a philanthropic gesture, but as a business proposition.

Tonik is a great illustration of what I call a *submarket* product or service: an innovative business strategy that is designed to make money by solving a social problem. Submarket means "beneath the market"—constituencies or geographies that are beyond the traditional focus of commercial enterprises. Submarket strategies, then, focus on developing specialized products and services for markets that previously were seen as impossible to address profitably. Submarkets can be geographic (for example, focused on inner-cities or developing countries) or "social" (that is, focused on social issues like hunger, health care, environment, or education).

What's unique about submarkets is not that their needs have been entirely ignored, but that they have been relegated almost exclusively to the domain of charity and government programs. Yet as round after round of government stimulus spending has proven, subsidies and charity cannot actually solve social problems; they just hold them at bay a bit longer. According to C. K. Prahalad and Stu Hart, "Foreign aid and charitable giving have not alleviated the problems for the world's poor. In the late 20th century, it has become clear that government is not up to the challenge of creating wealth for the masses."[10] Corporate philanthropists are coming to the same conclusion: social issues are becoming business issues, and social solutions increasingly require business solutions.

Sometimes the answer to social problems is business itself. Recently I was conducting some research for a large corporate foundation by interviewing some of the company's retail workers. I asked them which philanthropic issue they felt was most important for the company to support: hunger, homelessness, education, health care, and the like. Their unanimous answer: jobs! After all, most, if not all, of the social issues mentioned are symptoms of poverty, the remedy to which is most often employment. In many cases, this is the most obvious and organic way for companies to make a social impact. In other cases, companies can mobilize their resources, R&D strength, market power, or simply their own products to solve complex social issues in highly profitable ways.

The *Backstory*: How We Got Here

So how did submarket products and services come to be a viable business strategy? I have identified three key drivers: short-tail economics, bottom-of-the-pyramid-ization, and disruptive innovation. In the crucible of the social capital market, these forces have created great opportunities for social innovation. Let's take a closer look.

1. Short-Tail Economics

Today for $1 you can buy a double cheeseburger from Burger King, a five-layer beef burrito from Taco Bell, or a sausage Egg McMuffin from McDonald's. Even more unbelievable is the fact that these companies are able to make a profit selling these and other $1 products. Globalization and automation have dramatically lowered the cost of producing most commodity goods and services, to the point that companies can now sell them at miniscule prices and still earn a profit. It's what you might call "short-tail economics."

"Long-tail economics" was a concept coined by *Wired* magazine's Chris Anderson to illustrate how the Internet has made it possible for companies to sell large numbers of items in small quantities profitably (like custom-colored M&Ms). In an era without the constraints of physical shelf space and other distribution bottlenecks, narrowly targeted goods and services can be as economically attractive as mainstream fare.[11] The long-tail theory is based on an assumption—that consumers value extreme choice—and its correlate: our economy is shifting from mass market to millions of niches.

That may well be true. But what long-tail economics also reveals is that there is a *short tail* at the other end of the curve: a phenomenon wherein consumers seek mass quantities of fewer, more generic items, like basic clothing and personal care items. Think of it as extreme commoditization.[12] This has set the stage for submarket social innovation.

Short-tail economics is democratizing capitalism: increasing access to basic goods and services like food, clothing, and shelter, which once had to be subsidized by the government or nonprofits. A perfect illustration of a submarket product and service is Walmart's $4 generic prescription drug program, Although Walmart's aggressive pricing and market-making capability have given the company a bad rap in some circles, the company has also found ways to use its muscle to generate positive social impacts and profits.

But short-tail commoditization isn't just democratizing basic needs—it's also democratizing access to quality-of-life enablers like health care, education, and the availability of financial services. As America has become more affluent, we have increased our expectations of minimum standards for social welfare. Yesterday's luxuries are today's basic necessities. We're not quite at the point where the government will be handing out Louis Vuitton stamps, but there is a clear recognition that what it takes to sustain a life in modern society today is much more than it used to be. The fact that universal health care is a national entitlement in every industrialized nation except the United States validates this point. As a result, the focus of social change in the United States is increasingly aimed at economic security for the "working poor." Thus social innovation strategies are playing out on both levels: they're aimed at commoditizing basic needs and increasing access to quality-of-life services.

2. Bottom-of-the-Pyramid-ization

In 2000, a wave of publicity about the so-called "bottom of the pyramid" (or BOP) sparked a new era of commercial interest in social markets.[13] The BOP is the world's largest and poorest socio-economic group, comprising an estimated four billion people living on less than $2 per day; that's nearly two-thirds of the world's population. Many in the BOP live in rural villages and urban slums in India, East Africa, and other developing regions, often outside the reach of mainstream commerce. It is estimated that by the year 2050, 85 percent of consumers will live in developing nations.[14] As a result of all the BOP hype and some high-profile success stories, many corporations are beginning to wake up and smell the (fair trade) coffee. And it's not just the usual suspects (that is, large multinational corporations) that are getting into the game. For example, Amway (Alticor) is exploring possibilities for microfranchising in Ghana.

Pioneering research by business school professors C. K. Prahalad and Stu Hart has demonstrated how corporations, using the right strategies, can generate enormous profits by targeting the BOP. The archetypal example is Grameen Bank. Founded in 1983, Grameen is a for-profit bank that provides microcredit and tiny loans (averaging $15) to poor customers, enabling entrepreneurship, access to vital services, and an improved quality of life. The bank has been profitable almost every year since its inception and boasts a 97-percent loan recovery rate—the highest of any banking system in the world.

Although focus on the BOP has been a major driver of social innovation, BOP strategies are *not* synonymous with social innovation. Many BOP advocates argue that availing the poor of virtually any product or service is a good thing, be it one-cent shampoo, rural cell-phone service, or four-cent Cadbury chocolate. Social innovation, in contrast, is about using business ingenuity and the profit motive to develop solutions to social problems, some of which involve access to vital services. As such, submarket social innovation involves using corporate resources to solve social problems, not just to make money by selling to the poor. Still, the movement has stimulated interest in marrying social problems with business opportunities, and this has formed a powerful conceptual predicate for social innovation.

3. Disruptive Innovation

In 1995 Clay Christensen, a Harvard Business School professor, coined the term "disruptive innovation" to describe a new category of "good enough," low-cost products and services that were under-engineered to meet the basic needs of mass consumers.[15] These offerings are typically simpler, more convenient, and less expensive, so they appeal to new or less-demanding customers.[16] Southwest Airlines used low-cost, short-haul flights to disrupt the traditional airline industry. The PC computer disrupted the mainframe business with dramatically lower-cost, good-enough computing power. And the iPod disrupted the music industry with game-changing design, storage capacity and, well, just about everything.

More recently, Christensen broadened this idea to what he called "catalytic innovations" or good-enough solutions to social problems that had not been adequately addressed.[17] Christensen argues that innovation is inherently limited in the social sector because much of the money available to address social needs is given to organizations that are wedded to their current solutions, delivery models, and recipients.[18]

Christensen sees catalytic innovators as exhibiting the following characteristics:

1. They create systemic social change through scaling and replication; that is, they design the solution to be expanded quickly once it's successful in initial markets.
2. They meet a need that is either overserved (because the existing solution is more complex than many people require) or not served at all.
3. They offer products and services that are simpler and less costly than existing alternatives and may be perceived as having a lower level of performance, but users consider them to be good enough.
4. They generate resources, such as donations, grants, volunteer manpower, or intellectual capital, in

ways that are initially unattractive to incumbent
competitors.
5. They are often ignored, disparaged, or even encouraged
    by existing players for whom the business model is
    unprofitable or otherwise unattractive and who therefore
    avoid or retreat from the market segment.[19] (p. 3)

Christensen offers examples like MinuteClinics, which provides
inexpensive walk-in medical services to populations including the
uninsured, and Apex Learning's low-cost online language courses,
which provide more learning options for U.S. high school students.
Today, Christensen's notion of disruptive or catalytic innovation
falls under the broader umbrella of social innovation. Disruptive
innovation is one way to address the needs of submarkets by microfying products and services: creating "good enough" functionality
and dramatically reducing price to appeal to a larger audience.

Short-tail economics, bottom-of-the-pyramid-ization, and disruptive innovation all spring from the same mechanism: leveraging
market efficiencies to profit from market *inefficiencies*. Think about
it—short-tail economics enables companies to use highly efficient manufacturing to create low-cost commodities for inefficient,
underserved markets like the uninsured. BOP strategies leverage
market efficiencies in areas like finance to serve inefficient markets
like credit for the poor in developing countries. And disruptive
innovation leverages the market efficiency of scaling and replication to serve inefficient markets like nonprofits and social services.
The fact is, the only real opportunity for outsized growth in a fully
efficient market is through innovation. Hence the market opportunity for social innovation: it offers companies a powerful way of
beneficially exploiting their existing investments in R&D, products and services, and manufacturing. Social innovation through
submarket products and services may in fact be as much a salvation
for corporations as it is for the beneficiaries of social change!

Unlocking the value to submarkets requires something I call
"social arbitrage," or finding the gap in value between how the

market sees a particular social problem or constituency and the true economic potential of that opportunity. It's what Tonik and Wal-mart did for the uninsured. It's what many "green" entrepreneurs are doing for climate change. And what BOP companies are doing for international development. And it's what your company can do for many other submarkets yet to be discovered.

The *Formula*: How This Strategy Works

Succeeding with a submarket product or service strategy isn't as easy as it may seem. As one researcher observed, "Simply subtracting product features and raising advertising budgets to appeal to the low-income market is generally insufficient."[20] Thus social innovation strategies require a mix of insight, ingenuity, and determination.

Here are the five steps to making it work:

1. Identify the Social Problem That Makes Sense for Your Business to Address

Social issues directly affect every business today, and not just as a negative reputation risk that has to be "managed." To determine the issues that present the highest value potential for your business, it is important to ask the right questions. When you do, the right answer usually becomes obvious. When you ask the wrong questions, you get nowhere. One corporation I worked with recently conducted a survey asking its customers, "Which social issues are most important to you?" Here's just a sample of what they got back: child welfare, the environment, education, homelessness, veterans, senior citizens, breast cancer, juvenile diabetes ... everything! The point: focus your inquiry.

The key question you will need to answer is, which "submarket" offers the most potential value to our business? Here are some of the criteria to consider:

- *Economic potential:* What is the buying power of this market? For example, few realize the true extent of the

market for people with physical disabilities. People
with disabilities have $220 billion in discretionary
spending power.[21] Seventy-two percent of people with
disabilities are "likely to upgrade to a product's latest
model."[22] And travelers with disabilities spend
$4.2 billion on lodging and $3.3 billion on air travel
annually.[23]

- *Ripeness of need:* Is the market aware of its needs or
  deficiencies? For example, in 2009, a large direct-sales
  firm set out to sell products in Ghana. The company
  initially considered selling low-cost manual water
  pumps, as there was a scarcity of potable drinking
  water, only to find out that although that was true,
  the Ghanaians they interviewed didn't value clean
  water enough to pay for it rather than other life
  necessities.

- *Accessibility:* What are the physical, technical, or
  economic barriers to entry? As with any business
  opportunity, barriers to entry are important to assess.
  Does your company have the technology and processes
  to make the hypothetical product profitably? Can you
  distribute it to the target market easily?

- *Politics:* Are there reasons why this market may be
  politically beneficial or risky? For example, GE timed
  things right politically when it launched its
  healthymagination initiative on May 7, 2009 (just days
  before a major White House announcement on health
  care cost savings) and at a time when the health care
  market was heating up to be the nation's most
  high-profile social issue. At the other extreme, there
  may be issues or markets that are politically sensitive
  either for customers or your particular corporate culture

and therefore distracting to the social innovation
efforts.

- *Competitive landscape:* Are other firms already serving
  this niche? Although first-mover advantage can be
  significant, sometimes it can be a boon to act
  immediately after a high-profile failure or competitor's
  withdrawal from a market. For example, after a
  short-lived attempt by Zurich to sell micro-insurance to
  small entrepreneurs in Bolivia, Aon decided to launch
  an entirely different business model, selling innovative
  products like micropensions direct to entrepreneurs.
  The program was an immediate success: acquiring
  ninety thousand new clients in nineteen months and
  generating profit margins of 45 percent.

Remember that submarkets can be *geographic* or *social* in
nature. Examples of geographic submarkets include inner cities
or low-income neighborhoods, developing countries, or communities devastated by a natural disaster (such as New Orleans or Haiti).
Social submarkets may include the economically or socially disadvantaged (such as people with disabilities, certain minority groups,
illiterate adults, the uninsured, battered women), or social "industries" themselves: health care, education, the environment, human
services, and the like. In WellPoint's case, the company gauged the
economic, strategic, and political importance of the "uninsured" as
a submarket—specifically the young invincibles—and determined
that it was accessible, that there were few competitors serving that
market, and that the need was "ripe."

2. Understand and Address Unique Market Requirements

Every market has a secret code that's required to crack it. The
key is to do your sleuthing *before* rolling out a new product or
service to the submarket. That's how Tonik was so successful.
WellPoint did its homework: the company conducted in-depth,

one-on-one, reverse-point-of-view interviews and asked young people to keep a journal about their thoughts and experience with health care. What they discovered gave them the key to unlocking the market. First, WellPoint uncovered a crucial fact: that young invincibles weren't actually opposed to the concept of health insurance; they just felt that most policies didn't meet their needs and didn't fit their pocketbooks. Second, most young invincibles didn't have a history with group-sponsored plans, so they assumed that health insurance should cover everything: "Aren't my eyes part of my health?" one interviewee said.[24] One big takeaway was that this segment overanticipated the cost of insurance and underanticipated the cost of medical care—key trends to consider for WellPoint's products and marketing targeting this market. Finally, young invincibles were intimidated by all the legalese: deductibles, coinsurance, out-of-network coverage, and so on. The poor transparency deterred them from signing up.

Based on this information, WellPoint executives tailored a product and marketing campaign to suit the idiosyncratic needs they perceived for the young invincibles submarket. In short, WellPoint:

- *Redesigned the product,* making sure Tonik covered everything (that is, dental, vision, prescriptions), both to enhance perceptions of value and to keep things simple, with these exceptions: they excluded maternity benefits (given the segment's lack of interest in these) and brand-name prescriptions (to keep costs down).

- *Established a new customer acquisition/retention strategy* including a very hip, completely online marketing campaign—with a much more conversational tone and accessibility than typical insurance marketing tactics—and a separate customer service unit, again with a focus on online features.

- *Staged Tonik's rollout* carefully, starting with California and moving slowly to other states. They used the fifty-three thousand applications they received in 2006 to build momentum.[25]

In researching the needs of a submarket, sometimes you can also find important loopholes or gaps that make your product more appealing. For example, Walmart realized that their $4 generic drug plan was also attractive to Medicare recipients. Even though those prescriptions are ostensibly covered by the government, many enter the Medicare Part D coverage gap called the "doughnut hole": once an individual's drug cost for a given year reaches a threshold (currently $2,250), the beneficiary must pay out of pocket (currently up to $3,600) before government subsidies kick in again.[26] Walmart also designates one pharmacy associate per store to be a Medicare Part D expert who, in conjunction with its in-store informational kiosks, helps customers understand both the enrollment process and the benefits to which they are entitled.[27] These systems enabled the retailer to help enroll 1,080,000 people for the Medicare Part D prescription drug benefit, as of October 26, 2006.[28]

3. Innovate

This is the toughest part: coming up with the "Aha!" or intuitive leap that enables you to create a new submarket value proposition. There are a number of different ways companies can innovate submarket products and services. Here are the five most common methods:

- *Microfy.* The key to this type of innovation lies in the "20/80" rule: identifying the 20 percent of functionality that meets 80 percent of the need. That's what General Electric did with its lightweight electrocardiograph machine, the MAC 800.[29] The machine, which recently came on the U.S. market, includes the latest technology but at six pounds weighs half as much as the smallest ECG previously available. More importantly, the MAC 800 retails for just $2,500, 80 percent below the cost of machines with similar functionality. Not surprisingly, the target segments fit our submarket profile: primary care docs, rural clinics, and visiting nurses, who need portable devices but can't foot the bill for the more expensive machines.

The 20/80 rule also worked for Tonik: removing maternity coverage, one of the highest-cost items, allowed WellPoint to dramatically lower the price without forsaking the product's value. Walmart's $4 generic prescription plan is another illustration: generic drugs provide the same functionality of their brand-name counterparts at a fraction of the cost.[30] In fact, the FDA estimates that 50 percent of generic drugs are produced by brand-name firms![31]

Speaking about how the MAC 800 can serve as a model for other divisions of GE, John Rice, CEO of the company's Technology Infrastructure group, said, "Often, the trap is thinking that innovation is about making the next iPod or BlackBerry. But maybe it's a simpler, lower-cost version of those. The innovation in all of our businesses now is bringing costs down."[32] That's what microfying is all about: reducing a key element like cost while retaining the core value of the product or service and making it appealing to new markets.

- *Drive "core-competency" social innovation.* This is about transferring the business's core competencies, or existing know-how and business capabilities, to submarkets. In 2009, GE launched its *healthymagination* initiative to deliver what it calls "sustainable health care" by "combining technology with innovation and smarter processes" to bring "quality health care to more people at lower cost."[33] GE will spend $3 billion over the next six years on R&D to develop a hundred new health care innovations. In addition, GE will commit $2 billion of financing over the next six years to drive health care information technology and improve health care in rural and underserved areas, plus $1.5 billion for partnerships, content, and services. Make no mistake, this is not philanthropy, as GE makes clear: "It is a fundamental refocusing of how we invest in the business and the way we develop technology."[34] The company is expecting to make profits with the initiative, just as it would with offerings targeted to more traditional markets.

When asked how they conceived of *healthymagination*, executives referred to the notion of core competency social innovation: "There wasn't one specific 'aha' moment or one particular innovation which makes this strategy work. We think GE is very good at picking industry tipping points—just like we did with our green strategy, *ecomagination*."[35] The company explains: "When there is a convergence of social need, customer need, consumer preference, technology and policy in an industry like health care, we think we have the technology, the know-how and the dedication to drive change."[36]

GE is not alone. Many other firms are realizing the positive link between commercial technology and social impact. Salesforce.com is a leading technology firm that builds web-based customer-relationship management software. Although the firm focused initially on small and mid-sized companies, it soon realized that hundreds of nonprofits and social service agencies were jury-rigging its software for fundraising and constituent tracking. Salesforce.com then began offering free customized software to small nonprofits through its foundation, ultimately paving the way for a line of for-profit products aimed at meeting the needs of larger nonprofit, public sector, and education organizations at a fraction of the cost being charged by large, high-end software firms. In the words of one nonprofit enthusiast: "The 1.5 million community-serving organizations in the United States now have access to the same innovative technology tools used by the largest and most successful companies on the planet—and what's more is that it's possible for those tools to be practically implemented."[37] For Salesforce.com, that's a pretty significant social impact—and a new business market.

- *Use "trickle-up" innovation.* Although some companies are innovating by applying commercial lessons learned to submarkets, others are doing the reverse. It's called "trickle-up" innovation: a growing number of companies are testing out new products and services in alternative markets and then upstreaming successful ideas to more established markets. Again we use the example of GE's MAC 800 electrocardiograph machine. Rather than developing the scaled-down machine from scratch (which can take up to five years and cost $2 million), GE based it on the field model it developed for physicians in China and India in 2008.[38] Modifications of the field model included a twelve-button keypad to replace a full keyboard (saving costs) and the addition of USB, Ethernet, and telephone ports to upload patient readings (and satisfy the U.S. market, which is accustomed to such features). Using trickle-up innovation helped GE cut U.S. development costs to $225,000 and time-to-market to just months.

Trickle-up innovation doesn't always start in the developing world. WellPoint figured out how to segment and "flavorize" products for key demographics based on its learnings from Tonik. According to WellPoint executives, "Tonik was a good lesson on segmentation: for example, how can we serve the pre-retiree? What changes do they want in a product?"

- *Make it profitable.* As GE's CEO Jeff Immelt likes to say, "The most important part of corporate social responsibility is 'corporate'—you gotta make money, you gotta win."[39] And GE is winning. In 2008, GE's *ecomagination* strategy, which develops environmentally friendly technology like ultra-efficient "green" locomotives, generated revenues of $17 billion, up 21 percent from the prior year. More generally, what's not profitable is not sustainable. And what's not sustainable is not going to be around long enough to have any social impact. So if your model is designed right—that is, you've aimed your submarket product or service at effectively solving a social problem—then profits equal impact.

There are many ways companies can make submarket strategies profitable: take advantage of economies of scale, remove some frills, use alternative delivery mechanisms, cut out middlemen, find a way to tap federal funding streams. Walmart is a great case in point: the move to reduce generic prices was pure Walmart strategy—target the pockets of inefficiency in the system. Walmart got rid of third-party distributors, cut the profit margin, automated the distribution system, and reduced the inventory cycle. "It is not glamorous," said Bill Simon, an executive vice president at Walmart. "It's pennies at a time."[40] But pennies add up.

• *Think bigger—take submarket offerings to scale.* Social innovation strategies are business strategies; therefore submarket offerings should be scalable. Having a good idea is always important, but if the goal is to maximize profits and maximize social impact, scale matters. There are two ways to scale your innovation: by scope or by segment. In the case of Tonik, WellPoint is doing both. The product has now been rolled out to six states, and WellPoint is already considering variations of Tonik for other niche market segments. Walmart is scaling its innovation another way: the company is currently taking the $4 prescription plan to the next level, working directly with large employers like Caterpillar and others to lower health care costs for the more than seventy-five million employees whose employers fund their own health insurance plans. Could

Walmart ultimately provide low-cost health insurance direct to consumers? It's not out of the question.

The *Pitfalls*: What to Watch Out For

Here are some key tips on what to avoid in designing and implementing submarket product and service strategies.

1. It's Not Just About Microfying

Submarket products are not just about repackaging products in smaller bundles and selling at low prices to poor consumers in underdeveloped countries. They are about creating a new form of value. That means that you must understand both how the submarket values (or doesn't value) a particular product or service and the specialized needs of submarket segments. The way you create value—social arbitrage, if you will—isn't just by lowering costs, but also by innovating. If GE's MAC 800 ECG machine didn't have the key functionality target users needed, it wouldn't have sold well at any price point, not matter how low.

2. Submarket Doesn't Mean Low Quality

Tonik may be inexpensive, but it isn't cheap. Tonik customers' choice of providers isn't limited to a few HMO doctors: they have access to the entire Blue Cross PPO network in their state. GE's MAC 800 is no less reliable than its big-cousin, more expensive versions. And generic prescription drugs work just as well as their branded counterparts: the FDA requires generic drugs to have the same quality, strength, purity, and stability as brand-name drugs.[41]

3. Be Careful Not to Cannibalize

Sometimes you have to protect your core business. Philips Electronics, for example, considered taking the low-cost, solar-powered lighting it designed for Ghana and marketing it throughout the developed world. But CEO Gerard J. Kleisterlee has held off in order to avoid cannibalizing Philips's existing product line, explaining that "[you run the risk of] hurting margins if you go too far down."[42] The way to win is to create a distinct offering with a distinct value proposition to a distinct market. Salesforce.com limits its free nonprofit software to organizations with ten users or fewer, preserving its ability to generate profits from larger organizations.

Developing submarket products and services is more than a great social innovation—it's a critical business strategy for growth-seeking companies across sectors, from consumer goods to technology. Players in these and other industries have to create offerings that will serve the needs of untapped market segments that are both socially beneficial and economically robust. By microfying, using trickle-up innovation, and leveraging their core business in other ways, companies can use social strategies to extend their business proposition and expand their bottom line.

Chapter 5

STRATEGY TWO:
ENTER NEW MARKETS THROUGH
BACKDOOR CHANNELS

One way to grow your business is to use social innovation to invent new products and services; another is to use social innovation to invent new markets. Many of the largest and most lucrative business markets—geographic and demographic—are also the most mature (and competitive) markets. Yet the great untapped markets that remain—inner cities, developing countries, marginalized demographics, and other "sub-markets"—are often perceived as impenetrable, because they are either hard to reach, underdeveloped, undereducated, or all of these. The barriers to entering these markets are different from most: they are social barriers, not competitive barriers. In fact, these markets have virtually no competition. This chapter explains how companies like Tesco and Coca-Cola are using social innovation as a business strategy to overcome social barriers and turn orphaned markets into growth opportunities.

Tesco: Building Oases in the Food Desert

The store near two payday loan outlets and a Mexican butcher shop in Phoenix doesn't look like an oasis, but that's exactly what it is. Tesco's Fresh & Easy Neighborhood Markets are aimed at stranded communities, where fresh fruit and vegetables don't exist for miles around. These areas are becoming popularly known as "food deserts."[1] Tesco, a UK-based company and the world's third-largest food retailer, is using the new smaller convenience stores (ten thousand square feet on average) to penetrate the U.S. market for the first time in its hundred-year history. In fact, few British retailers have ever succeeded in the United States, so when Tesco announced in February 2006 that it would invest $472 million per year to establish a beachhead in the United States, it was a big gamble.[2] But Tesco had a plan, and it involved entering a new market through backdoor channels, or "backdoor market entry."

Instead of taking the market head-on, Tesco made its entry into the United States by going after an orphaned market riddled with social issues but offering a big financial prize. So far, the strategy has gone according to plan. As of late 2009, the company had opened 129 stores, primarily in Phoenix, Las Vegas, and Southern California.[3] According to the most recent management report in late 2009, Tesco expects to open additional U.S. stores at a rate of around one per week through 2010—even in the wake of a dramatic recession! As of late 2009, U.S. sales were up 115 percent, with revenues of $260,000,000.[4] The operation is still in the red due to startup costs, but the company is meeting investor expectations.

Tesco did its homework, studying the U.S. market for almost twenty years, looking for the right way in. What the company came up with, Fresh & Easy Neighborhood Markets, not only targeted areas of cities largely ignored by U.S. grocers but also allowed Tesco to avoid competing with retail giants like Walmart. According to a retail industry analyst, "Big supermarket operators tend to locate at out-of-town or edge of town locations. You can't slap a store of 80,000 square feet slap in the middle of Phoenix or Los Angeles."[5] To stick to the health-focused theme, Fresh & Easy doesn't sell cigarettes or many foods with trans fats or additives—unlike Tesco's British outlets. The stores are good for the environment, too, using green technology like solar panels.

And half the products carried are private label (Fresh & Easy's own brand), promoting higher profit margins.[6]

Food deserts are a major health threat in the United States and other developed countries like Britain, which house a growing number of densely populated, low-income, inner-city communities that lack grocery stores with fresh and healthy food options. More than twenty-three million Americans, including six and a half million children, live in low-income urban and rural neighborhoods that are more than a mile from a supermarket.[7] These locales are replete with "fringe food" outlets: fast-food franchises, mom-and-pop burger joints, and convenience stores that rarely offer healthy options such as fresh fruit and vegetables. Solving this problem is obviously of paramount importance to the community, local government, and health advocates. The issue also presents a powerful market entry strategy for nontraditional food retailers, especially when many traditional food retailers like Walmart, Costco, and SuperTarget have faced political and other barriers to entering such urban markets.

By aiming their business at this social problem, Tesco not only has found a way into the U.S. market, but also has positioned itself to have a major social impact. Researchers found that Tesco's experience in addressing food deserts in the UK had an impact on public health, particularly those who had had the least healthy diets when they switched from a limited discounter to Tesco.[8] Building on these results, Tesco has announced plans to locate new outlets in the areas most needing them, such as South L.A. This is good news for communities desperate for healthy food options—and great PR for Tesco. Tim Mason, head of Tesco's U.S. operations, explained, "One of the reasons we appeal to American politicians is because we have said we will go back into neighborhoods that have become 'food deserts.'"[9] So the food deserts, a major problem in the United States, have become a way for Tesco to enter a new market, helping the retailer grow while promoting positive social change.

The *Innovation*: Why This Strategy Works

Tesco is a perfect illustration of the innovation strategy I call "backdoor market entry"—that is, forging new market inroads through the gateway of social change. But entering many of the remaining untapped markets requires a lot of ingenuity and some tricky maneuvering. Increasingly the biggest barriers to infiltrating new markets are not political or cultural, but social: unskilled workers, poverty, illiteracy, disenfranchised women, limited access to vital services, poor infrastructure, resource deficiencies, and the like. Companies can leverage their capabilities to solve these problems as a legitimate means of entering new markets.

For example, businesses can use backdoor market entry to enhance relationships with governments in target markets, dovetailing their desire for growth with ways of addressing the social needs of local communities. This is vastly different from sprinkling around some charity dollars to provide political air cover. It's about using your core business to create social change. And it's applicable in any kind of market.

Coca-Cola illustrates use of the backdoor market entry strategy in the developing world. And its vehicle for the strategy has two wheels and sometimes comes with a bell. Yes, a bicycle is a key element of the beverage behemoth's international distribution. With overseas markets driving 80 percent of the company's profits today, continued growth abroad is essential. But getting into these markets poses many challenges—sometimes it's the lack of infrastructure; sometimes it's the politics; sometimes it's the workforce. In Coke's case, it was all three. Coke's traditional hub-and-spoke distribution wouldn't work in many countries, especially those with many consumers living in densely populated or hard-to-reach, remote locations. For example, Coca-Cola executives knew that in order to expand the company's reach into East Africa's high-density urban areas, they couldn't rely on having bottling partners drop limited quantities of product at thousands of small retail outlets. They had to come up with a new, more customized distribution system. And they found just what they needed at one of their distributors: Coca-Cola Sabco (which stands for "South African Bottling Company").

To expand its market share in East Africa, Sabco had innovated a model they called the Manual Distribution Center (MDC). The MDC model uses small businesses (increasingly first-time entrepreneurs and women) to deliver Coca-Cola products manually to local small-scale retailers. Because these areas are often beyond the reach of delivery trucks, MDCs often use bicycles and pushcarts to deliver their products. The benefit is mutual: Sabco grows its distribution, and local communities benefit from new jobs and wealth creation.[10] Sabco rolled out the MDC model as a pilot in 1999, using ten MDCs in Addis Ababa, Ethiopia. Over the next decade, the MDC model spread widely through Coke's East Africa markets. As of November 2008 there were approximately 165 MDCs in Addis Ababa and 651 across Ethiopia—each covered about 150 retail outlets—accounting for 83 percent of Sabco sales nationwide. There were 152 MDCs in Dar es Salaam and 412 across Tanzania, accounting for 93 percent of Sabco sales nationwide. Where used, the MDC business model can account for up to 95 percent of total volume.[11] Based largely on this success, the MDC model is now the core distribution model in many parts of Africa, including Ethiopia, Kenya, Uganda, Mozambique, Tanzania, and, to a smaller extent, Namibia.[12] Overall, Coca-Cola has created over 2,500 MDCs in Africa; these currently employ over 12,000 people and generate over $500 million in annual revenues.[13] Plans call for the creation of an additional 1,500 to 2,000 MDCs, which could generate as many as 8,400 jobs and another half billion dollars in revenue over the next three years.

The MDC model has been so successful not only because it solves an important distribution problem for Coca-Cola but also because it produces immediate, substantial benefits for targeted communities. According to Coca-Cola, the model "has created jobs, promoted entrepreneurship and strengthened local economies."[14] Let's look at some of the hard evidence for the MDC's social impact:[15]

- *Entrepreneurship:* In Ethiopia, 75 percent of MDC owners are "new business owners," with 80 percent of these relying on the MDC as their sole income source.

- *Employment:* In Ethiopia and Tanzania alone, the MDC model has created over six thousand jobs. In Tanzania, each MDC employs nearly seven people, on average.

- *Income:* In Ethiopia, 95 percent of MDC owners and 80 percent of staff say that they "make more money now" than before.

- *Empowerment:* In Tanzania, 35 percent of owners are female, and over 40 percent of MDCs employed at least one female. In Ethiopia, over 80 percent of MDC owners and pushcart operators reported receiving training.

A *BusinessWeek* article summed up the benefits of Coke's MDC model well: "This is the kind of corporate program that can have a huge impact on struggling economies and, over time, create vast new markets for products and services. It's a great example of how some corporations are shifting their CSR strategies. Rather than spreading money around to good causes, which may or may not have a lot of impact, they're doing what they do best: business."[16]

The *Backstory*: How We Got Here

Why does using backdoor market entry work as a social innovation strategy? Several trends have made this strategy more valuable for—and even expected of—major businesses.

1. Barriers to Entry Are Increasingly Social

Beyond the usual suspects (such as capital investment, brand identity, switching costs, and entrenched competition), social and political factors are increasingly the swing variable in entering new markets. Social barriers include poverty (for example, limited purchasing power), literacy (for example, lack of local talent and skilled labor), limited social awareness (for example, of the importance of clean drinking water or hand washing), disenfranchisement (of women or minorities), limited access to vital services (such as health care, financing, Internet access), poor infrastructure (for example, lack of roads, housing, or electricity) or environmental resource deficiencies (such as a lack of energy or water). These issues aren't just in emerging markets like Africa and India; they're in our own backyard too—social barriers affect urban markets like Detroit, Newark, and the South Side of Chicago as well as rural areas like those in Appalachian Ohio. To surmount these barriers, corporations are turning to more sophisticated market entry strategies that solve social problems *as part of a market entry strategy.* These strategies can be designed to enhance local standards of living, develop talent, stimulate entrepreneurship, eradicate disease, build social marketing platforms, and deepen relationships with governments.

Academics, politicians, and management gurus have been touting the advantages of untapped "social" markets for years. In an *Inc.* magazine article from 1995, Harvard Business School professor and strategy guru Michael Porter argues that inner-city markets offer companies many strategic advantages: location (near high-rent business centers and public transportation hubs), local market demand (high population density driving strong purchasing power), integration with regional clusters (proximity to key industries often housed in downtown areas, including financial services), and human resources (a large pool of potentially loyal entry-level employees).[17] Former U.S. president Bill Clinton, on a tour of inner-city neighborhoods near the end of his term, noted, "If you have people who want to go to work and people with money to spend and they're both in the same place, it's a good place to invest."[18] And most recently, First Lady Michelle Obama has called for eliminating food deserts within seven years as part of the Let's Move! campaign to fight childhood obesity.[19]

2. Interest in Private Sector Engagement Is Growing

In the past, some corporations may have thought of government as regulators and nonprofits as charities. But today they're viewed as business partners. The link between solving social problems and business expansion has never been greater. Governments are even providing financial incentives for companies to get into the game: just this year the White House announced a new Healthy Food Financing Initiative—a partnership between the U.S. departments of Treasury, Agriculture, and Health and Human Services that will invest $400 million a year to help bring grocery stores to underserved areas and help places such as convenience stores and bodegas carry healthier food options.[20] Public-private partnerships now span issues relating to global development, race relations, health care, and nuclear nonproliferation. In the United States and abroad, governments are offering corporate-friendly policies, tax incentives, and contracts to encourage the private sector to help solve social problems.

This is no surprise, given the growing power of big business. In the 1960s and 1970s, about two-thirds of foreign aid came from the government; today, over 80 percent comes from the private sector.[21] Based on the potential of such collaboration, the Obama administration has even created the nation's first "public-private partnership czar": in the summer of 2009, Elizabeth Bagley became the first Special Representative for the U.S. Department of State's Global Partnership Initiative.[22] Similarly, the Clinton Global Initiative (CGI) program, founded by the former president in 2005, was launched specifically to bring government groups, corporations,

NGOs, and others together to address global social issues. CGI's annual meetings have brought together over one hundred current and former heads of state, along with Nobel Peace Prize winners, hundreds of CEOs, philanthropists, and NGO directors. CGI members have made commitments worth $57 billion; these commitments have already improved the lives of over 200 million people in 150 countries.[23]

3. Philanthropy Has Its Limits

Philanthropy alone is insufficient to achieve business objectives. In a recent McKinsey survey, over 80 percent of respondents believed their philanthropic initiatives weren't completely effective for achieving objectives including competitive differentiation, risk management, and employee recruitment.[24] As I mentioned in Chapter Three, Corporate Social Innovation, strategic philanthropy has certain legal (self-dealing) and structural (grants to nonprofits) limitations that restrict its usefulness in generating business value. And although philanthropic investments in education, health, environment, and other areas may ultimately enhance a company's "competitive context," the potential benefits of these strategies to a company's market entry are indirect at best, and very long term.

Take Exxon Mobil Corp.'s experience in Africa, for example. As part of a high-stakes market entry strategy, Exxon, Chevron, BP, and others have been tripping over themselves to make charitable donations to hot new African oil markets, like Angola's. The companies have been funding everything from schools to CT scanners to malaria prevention and even solar energy systems. But requests for grant dollars quickly became never-ending, and many resulted in public relations headaches or uncomfortable entanglements in local politics. For example, even after Exxon paid to double the size of an Angolan school, the school principal asked for a bus, an electric generator, and laboratory supplies including microscopes and a centrifuge. "Exxon is like a father," he was quoted as saying. "A father who likes to give is a father we're going to ask a lot."[25] The imbroglio, chronicled by the *Wall Street Journal*, pointed out the difficulties of using charity as a business strategy.[26] When it comes to philanthropy, more is never enough.

Nor is philanthropy sustainable. In hard economic times, corporate philanthropy budgets decline. Sixty-one percent of companies surveyed in 2009 had already reduced their giving budgets, or were considering it, and 57 percent said that they are making or considering making fewer grants.[27] Philanthropy is not, nor will it ever be, a core competency for companies. As one Exxon community relations manager said, "We are an oil company. We are not the Red Cross."[28]

The *Formula*: How This Strategy Works

There are several key steps to making a backdoor market entry strategy work.

1. Identify Social Barriers and Opportunities

Backdoor entry requires more than a cursory scan of local social or environmental issues. Companies need to get on the ground to really understand what's going on. A crack team of Tesco operatives has spent the past two years conducting forensic research in the U.S. market, setting up a dummy store on a Los Angeles film set and even staying overnight with American families (sixty in all) to study how they live.[29] The company asked families to keep a diary for two weeks while they looked into their cupboards to understand how American consumers lived their lives. This is similar to the research that WellPoint conducted before rolling out Tonik to the young invincibles (as discussed in Chapter Four, Create Revenues Through Submarket Products and Services).

In another case, in planning a market entry strategy for Ghana, representatives from one of the world's largest direct-selling companies spent six months building understanding, trust, and, in their words, "empathy" with local community members. They asked important questions: *What are the most pressing needs in the community: hygiene, nutrition, helping families, others? How do people do business here? How do products and money trade hands?* The findings were highly informative. It turns out that in Ghana, one of the highest-value products was lighting. Moreover, what locals cared about more than actual cash flow was a steady salary—getting a monthly paycheck was a status symbol because it showed you had a real job.

There's no substitute for getting out in the field and meeting with a full range of stakeholders to understand the social barriers you'll face—and the best ways of overcoming them. In the words of one firm, it's all about "market intuition." So make sure to build that.

2. Tie Social Value to Your Core Business

The real power in backdoor market entry isn't about doing good—it's about creatively linking your *core* business to positive social change. Green strategies have proven the power of this combination, generating natural incentives for businesses to want to do more. Addressing the urban food-desert problem with healthy food options is a logical move for Tesco, because they already specialize in distributing a large selection of grocery products (including nutritious products) quickly to retail stores all over the nation, including urban areas. Similarly, the direct-seller in Ghana just cited makes a living by empowering local entrepreneurs to sell their products to their social networks. To succeed in Ghana, the company must economically empower local women, which includes teaching them business fundamentals.

Coca-Cola used a social impetus—its commitment to meeting the Millennium Development Goals (a set of global development and anti-poverty objectives agreed to by a large group of world leaders at the UN in 2000)—to expand its MDC model. The company enhanced the social impact (and business value) of the model by partnering with the International Finance Corporation and Harvard's Kennedy School to identify key opportunities for program enhancement, including more targeted recruitment of MDC owners and employees, optimized financing, and expanded training in its distribution network.[30] Each of these strategies has not only made a social impact but also boosted the expansion of Coke's business in the region.

The key to backdoor market entry innovation is to develop strategies that make possible unlikely business expansion by overcoming social barriers to entry. There are many ways to create social and business value through market entry; here are three of the most common:

- *Create distribution and jobs.* Creating jobs isn't particularly innovative, but creating jobs by empowering disadvantaged people is. At the end of the 1990s, Hindustan Unilever (the Indian subsidiary of the consumer packaged goods giant Unilever) recognized that the best way to expand its markets was to find a way to reach millions of potential consumers in remote villages where there is no retail distribution network, no advertising coverage, and poor roads and transport.[31] To do so, Unilever engineered a social innovation—combining its economic interest in tapping new markets with the social impact of empowering poor Indian women and single mothers to become micro-entrepreneurs.

  To scale quickly, Unilever tapped into a far-flung network of existing women's self-help groups formed to support microcredit schemes. Unilever identified, recruited, and trained Shakti ("strength" in Hindi) entrepreneurs from these groups to be their local sales representatives.[32] These representatives went door to door selling Unilever products that were specially reengineered for this low-income market, such as small packets of shampoo and other health, nutrition, and hygiene products.

Today, Unilever's Shakti initiative is forty-five-thousand entrepreneurs strong, serving a hundred thousand villages and representing nearly a hundred million consumers. The revenues generated are now close to $100 million annually, with margins very similar to those achieved through mainstream distribution channels. In the words of Unilever's CEO Patrick Cescau, "Make no mistake. Shakti is not a philanthropic activity. It is a serious and profitable business proposition."

• *Increase access to social products or services.* Another way to innovate is to find creative ways to leverage the business platform to increase access to vital products and services. For example, an international nonprofit called ColaLife is in early-stage discussions with Coke to open up their distribution channels in developing countries to carry "social products" such as oral rehydration salts (to mitigate dehydration related to diarrhea) and vitamin A tablets to people who need them desperately. ColaLife envisions incorporating an "aidpod" with these products into Coca-Cola crates that are carried throughout the MDCs.[33]

• *Create new supply chains.* Another way to create social impact by entering markets is to build local supply chains in ways that advantage your business. This is what Tesco did when it entered the United States. Because the grocer had to build its distribution network from scratch, it wound up sourcing 60 percent of its products locally—doing a great service to local farmers but also significantly reducing transportation and storage costs in its supply chain. Cummins is doing the same thing in Africa: creating a "human" supply chain to service its diesel engines. Without trained locals to service and maintain its products, Cummins would not succeed in these new markets.

3. Find a Credible Partner

This is the age of public-private partnerships: at last count, four-teen U.S. federal agencies have created public-private partnership strategies, including the departments of Labor, Commerce, Defense, and State, the U.S. Agency for International Development, even NASA! There are many advantages to these partnerships in facilitating market entry, including instant credibility, local con-nections, and sometimes even financial support. One executive told me, "NGOs are well-connected, and if they see a win-win, they'll make introductions for you and give you the credibility to move quickly."[34] Especially today, policymakers and nonprofits fully accept that companies have a profit motive, but they will refuse a partnership if there is no clearly related social change. An official with one federal agency told me the story of a law firm that proposed a partnership with the U.S. government to introduce the firm to local officials in an emerging market; in return, the firm would offer one hundred hours of pro bono assistance to local nonprofits. It was quickly rejected, as the social impact was purely gratuitous.

A more meaningful partnership is the one that Tesco developed with the California city of Compton to introduce its forty-third Fresh & Easy store. Compton has been working hard to overcome its reputation as poverty-ridden gang turf (it is best known as the birthplace of the Crips and the Bloods street gangs) and also to address a major food desert problem. Attracting fresh quality grocers had been nearly impossible until Tesco showed up. Under the leadership of Mayor Eric Perrodin, the city worked closely with Tesco executives to build the new store in less than a year.[35] Fresh & Easy soon became the centerpiece of the mayor's redevelopment strategy. Not only will the store provide a sorely needed grocery store for the community, along with new jobs, but it will also add about $200,000 annually in property tax payments to the city's coffers.[36]

Some innovative partnerships are designed to scale, producing even greater social and economic benefits. Unilever's Lifebuoy brand soap cofounded Global Handwashing Day and united with other members of the Global Public Private Partnership for Hand-washing (including UNICEF, the World Bank, and Procter & Gamble) to promote a single life-saving message: wash your hands with soap.[37] The social impact is stark: diarrhea and pneumonia claim the lives of more than 3.5 million children under age five.[38] It's believed that hand washing with soap could cut deaths from diarrhea by half and deaths from acute respiratory infections such as pneumonia by a quarter.[39] Global Handwashing Day now takes place in more than eighty-five countries worldwide, including many of Unilever's key markets (Unilever leads GHD activities in twenty-three countries).[40] In Sri Lanka, one million children pledged to wash their hands with the correct technique, with the help of public health inspectors, UNICEF, and Lifebuoy. In South Africa, Lifebuoy teamed up with the Department of Water Affairs; in Singapore, Lifebuoy forged a relationship with the Health Promotion Board and the World Toilet Organization to deliver widespread hygiene education in schools. In Indonesia, a mass public event hosted by Lifebuoy with ministers of health and education aimed to get thousands of school children to take hand-washing pledges that could save their lives.[41] In Bangladesh, the initiative set a Guinness world record, with more than fifty thousand people simultaneously washing their hands.[42] It's a great example of social innovation at work: Lifebuoy has become one of Unilever's fastest-growing brands in the personal care category and was voted one of India's most trusted brands.[43] Through its hand-washing initiatives, Lifebuoy ultimately intends to change the hygiene behavior of one billion people globally by the year 2015.[44]

There are many different types of potential partners—governments, NGOs, and the like. But remember to choose the most *credible* ones in the target market. When McDonald's sought a partner in China (see Chapter Eight, Influence Policy Through Reverse Lobbying, for more details), the company joined up with the Soong Ching Ling Foundation to execute its social strategy. The foundation, named for the late honorary president of the People's Republic of China, had decades of experience and was closely associated with the Chinese government. But in Russia, for example, a government-related partner might not be as useful, as citizens may see such collaborations as propaganda. Pay careful attention to the affiliations most valued—they may even be with celebrities, athletes, or other national figures, rather than the usual suspects like governments and nonprofits.

The *Pitfalls*: What to Watch Out For

Entering new markets is never easy, and sometimes social issues can complicate things further. Here are three common mistakes companies need to avoid making when using backdoor market entry strategies.

1. Don't Fall Into the Philanthropy Trap

It's easy to leave out the innovation and fall back on philanthropy, especially when partners may be asking for grants or financial support. That may well be part of a backdoor market entry strategy, but charity is not at the core. As the Tesco, Lifebuoy, Coke, and other examples demonstrate, charity is not always required for some of the greatest social impacts. These companies mobilized other noncash resources that they had in far greater abundance—their supply chains, distribution networks, and marketing prowess, and their business footprints—to create *business strategies* that deliver significant social value. It takes ingenuity, market insight, and a lot of research to get it right. And, as the Exxon example highlighted earlier proves, philanthropy isn't always easier.

2. Think Beyond the Bottom of the Pyramid

There has been a lot of publicity about the markets of India and Africa in recent years, buoyed by the hype surrounding the bottom of the pyramid. These are certainly worthy markets, but they are not the only worthy untapped markets. Backdoor market entry can work in any market, even the United States. Food deserts are just one example, but there are many other markets where backdoor market entry innovations—like creating distribution networks, access to vital products and services, and new supply chains—can generate tremendous impact (and business growth). Spend the time to research the market opportunities that may not appear obvious; they may well be the most valuable.

3. Be Careful Not to Overpromise and Underdeliver

Social issues often garner high-profile media coverage, and this can cut both ways. If you're going to take on a problem and commit business resources to doing so, make sure you follow through—because everyone's watching. Although Tesco has been criticized by some for not opening stores in enough low-income markets and avoiding discussions with trade unions, the company has been true to its word. Fresh & Easy pays $10 an hour—$1.50 more than the minimum wage where it does business—and offers employees health insurance, unlike some rivals.[45] The company also invited hundreds of applicants to attend job fairs at local YMCAs and worked hard to hire from local neighborhoods.[46] Amanda Shaffer of the Urban and Environmental Policy Institute at Occidental College in Los Angeles notes, "If it's really all that it has been advertised as … then they will be successful. If it turns out that it is just really impressive marketing that covers up a business that is not much different from its competitors … then the American public will figure it out in a while."[47]

Commenting on Coke's MDC strategy, Jane Nelson of Harvard's Kennedy School said, "There is a growing recognition in the corporate and international development communities that the most sustainable contribution companies can make to poverty alleviation is to carry out their core business activities in a profitable, responsible and inclusive manner."[48] To adopt this strategy, find points of connection between your core business and a specific social issue in an underserved market that it makes sense for you to target. Then match ways of solving the problem with something your business excels at, whether creative distribution models (like Coca-Cola), workforce development (like Unilever Shakti), or small-format grocery (like Tesco). Soon what appears to be a backdoor strategy may well become a gateway to enviable profits—and lasting social impact.

Chapter 6

STRATEGY THREE:
BUILD EMOTIONAL BONDS
WITH CUSTOMERS

So far we have explored using submarket offerings and backdoor market entry to drive profits and social impact. Although both of those can improve a company's reputation with potential customers and other groups, the strategy in this chapter is about a powerful new form of customer loyalty I call *emotive customer bonding*. This social innovation is about leveraging the customer experience to address meaningful social problems, and in so doing, building an almost familial allegiance to your brand. In today's commoditized, undifferentiated world of goods and services, the value of adding a "soul" to a brand is priceless.

OfficeMax's A Day Made Better

The Hills reality TV star Audrina Partridge went back to high school in the fall of 2009. She wasn't there to take classes: Audrina was delivering over $1,000 of free school supplies to her former teacher Cozette Pettit on behalf of OfficeMax. It was part of the company's three-year-old initiative, A Day Made Better (ADMB).

The program has one simple objective: eliminate the need for teachers to buy their own classroom supplies (what OfficeMax refers to as "teacher-funded classrooms").

Before starting ADMB, OfficeMax had asked customers what social issue was most important for the company to focus on. "Education" was the overwhelming answer. When OfficeMax discovered how much money teachers were spending out of their own pockets for school supplies—about $4 billion a year[1]—the company wanted both to raise awareness of the problem and to provide free supplies to teachers across America. Out of this idea was born ADMB.

In 2009, OfficeMax targeted about 1,200 U.S. schools through ADMB, with another 100 covered by the company's Mexico and Canada operations.[2] On October 1 of that year, about four thousand OfficeMax employee-volunteers visited targeted classrooms to surprise teachers and students with the free supplies (worth about $1,200, on average), which included classroom staples like paper and pencils, along with bigger-ticket items like digital cameras, supply carts, and swivel chairs. OfficeMax partnered with Adopt-a-Classroom, a 501(c)(3) organization that matches donors with classrooms to offset the personal expenses that teachers incur to ensure basic supplies for their classrooms. Adopt-a-Classroom helped OfficeMax identify deserving schools near a thousand OfficeMax locations and recruit worthy teachers. Along with Audrina Partridge, actress-director Penny Marshall visited her old school to deliver the supplies personally; other celebrities—Dakota Fanning, Dustin Hoffman, and Jessica Simpson, to name a few—showed their support by sending their favorite teacher a special gift.[3]

OfficeMax designed ADMB to benefit the business by making a positive social impact. OfficeMax saw ADMB as a way to "inspire a national movement of grassroots support for teachers."[4] Naturally, the schools targeted appreciated the program. According to an elementary school principal in Miami, Florida, "A Day Made Better improves teacher morale, provides more supplies for our children and our classrooms, and ultimately impacts the quality of education we offer."[5] But the data speaks for itself: an 832-percent increase in new classroom adoptions by Adopt-a-Classroom, and a huge boost to public awareness of teacher-funded classrooms via 150 broadcast news stories and 125 print and online outlets, resulting in 44.6 million audience impressions (that is, the estimated number of people the media coverage reached).[6]

The numbers are of course important, but so is what drives them. "We do this campaign because it really is helping thousands of unsung community heroes,"[7] says Bill Bonner, OfficeMax's senior director of external relations. And that high-profile help inspires strong emotional connections to the effort across a wide range of groups, leading to multiple business benefits. ADMB was designed to target both OfficeMax's largest market—education—and a specific, prototypical customer: "Eve." Eve is the thirty- or forty-something woman who purchases office supplies—typically a mom, a teacher, or both—with an eye on "everyday value."[8] Eve cares deeply about education and is a fan of efforts to improve education in a meaningful way. As Bonner says, "[P]eople look for genuine efforts and will endorse programs they can believe in."[9]

Thus ADMB was designed to create an emotional connection with the thousands of Eves that drive much of the market for office supplies, boosting OfficeMax's visibility, share, and revenues. For example, in the month after ADMB, OfficeMax's dedicated website for the program attracted sixteen thousand visits, 79 percent of which were unique.[10] According to OfficeMax, one indicator of the program's success on this dimension was the redemption of coupons included in brochures provided as part of ADMB, which generated at least "six figures of revenue at a profitable margin."[11] Similarly, OfficeMax won several bid contracts with school districts as a direct result of ADMB—the program gave them an edge over other bidders. One associate reported that the principal of the school her team went to had even offered to network with other principals to urge them to work with OfficeMax. And another team said that the teacher they surprised admitted she had been a Staples customer, but would now be a "loyal OfficeMax customer" who would recruit others to shop there.

But customers—including consumers and schools—weren't the only group ADMB was designed to affect. For OfficeMax employees, selling paper, pencils, and paper clips takes on much more meaning when their core business is linked to a powerful social impact. Thus OfficeMax involved thousands of employees directly and indirectly in ADMB, from packing boxes of supplies to delivering them to the teachers on the day of the event. The company also enabled senior managers, store managers, distribution managers, and others to adopt teachers through Adopt-a-Classroom, using several thousand online gift certificates. OfficeMax found clear evidence of ADMB's hoped-for impact on employees: 85 percent reported that the program improved camaraderie on their team; 94 percent believed it strengthened the company's community relationships; 99 percent said ADMB made them proud to work at OfficeMax.[12] As one employee noted, "I have been with OfficeMax for over twenty-five years, and this program is by far the most impressive thing we have ever done." The company recognized, of course, that enhanced satisfaction leads to happier and more productive employees. In fact, one of the initial motivations for ADMB was to integrate a fragmented workforce after the company's challenging merger with Boise-Cascade. Mission accomplished.

Given these far-reaching benefits in both social and business domains, ADMB, now an annual event, has become synonymous with OfficeMax's brand and culture, rather than just a one-time promotional campaign. In fact, when OfficeMax made major cuts in company budgets due to the 2008–09 recession, one initiative was untouched: ADMB. The company recognized the deep value the program has brought to its target market and the company itself by forging deep emotional connections to ADMB and OfficeMax more broadly, all while addressing an important social problem.

The *Innovation*: Why This Strategy Works

The social innovation strategy of building emotive customer bonds is the future of brand marketing: building a deeper sense of purpose for the brand, the customer experience, and the broader company as a whole by engaging social problems. The economic downturn has reshuffled the deck of customers for many companies. Some, like Walmart, have acquired hundreds of thousands of new customers as a result of a new value-conscious ethos in this country.[13] Others have seen significant customer attrition or more tenuous customer loyalty. In both cases, customer retention, not acquisition, is the new ground zero in the battle over the customer. To win, research by Gallup and others has shown that marketers "want to move beyond customer 'retention,' which is merely a behavior, to generating customer 'commitment,' 'delight,' and even 'evangelism'—all of which represent enduring psychological bonds that link a customer to a company."[14] Emotional connections are the lynchpin.

But forging emotional connections—particularly around nonemotional products or services like laundry detergent, banking, technology, or office supplies—is not easy. Companies are looking beyond traditional marketing interfaces and product attributes to seek out new methods for establishing psychic connections. Good customer service and smart packaging can get you only so far. Imbuing a company, or brand, with social meaning has become powerful glue in forging customer bonds. This is nothing new: in 2008 companies spent over $1.5 billion on cause marketing.[15] But it's no longer enough just to "associate" with a good cause—even one that makes sense for your company (for example, Kraft Foods and hunger). Emotion requires intensity, and intensity requires deep, meaningful engagement. That's where emotive customer bonding as a social innovation strategy is having its greatest impact.

The attributes that make this strategy work (and distinguish it from run-of-the-mill cause marketing) are also the very hallmarks of social innovation:

- *Has a clear business objective:* It's got to drive real return on investment (ROI) and focus on a key business priority. A short-lived sales promotion is not going to affect customer loyalty.

- *Leverages the core business:* The best bonds are the ones that use the primary engine of the business to solve a social problem. This is where the locus of impact is most significant.

- *Creates new value:* This strategy uses emotional connections to tap into latent value in the social capital market—in the case of OfficeMax, creating customer loyalty and employee discretionary effort.

- *Makes a meaningful social impact:* Donating $.10 to Charity X doesn't cut it anymore; to make a meaningful bond, it's got to make a meaningful difference.

Done right, this can be powerful stuff. Take, for example, McDonald's Ronald McDonald House program. The houses offer a "home away from home" for families who wish to stay near their critically ill children during treatment at nearby hospitals. I recall speaking to a family after they stayed at the Ronald McDonald House in Portland. They told me: "This place literally saved our lives … we are so thankful … we'll never eat at any other restaurant for the rest of our lives!" I call them "golden customers." And all told, through the families served by Ronald McDonald Houses®, Ronald McDonald Care Mobiles®, and Ronald McDonald Family Rooms®, McDonald's creates more than four million golden customers each year![16] Now, consider that the average person on Facebook has 110 friends,[17] and even if families served by McDonald's programs tell only 10 percent of their closest friends, the company has potentially created an emotional bond with over forty-four million people. That's a lot of love, and a lot of customer loyalty!

OfficeMax has created a similarly powerful emotional connection through its ADMB strategy, touching hundreds of thousands of lives. Exclaimed one teacher: "It's *better* than Christmas—this is awesome!" How likely are the teachers served by ADMB to shop anywhere but OfficeMax for office supplies? What about their same-school colleagues or even others—teachers and community members at large—who hear about their good fortune from them or catch a story about ADMB on their local news?

And don't forget, the emotional connection isn't just to customers. OfficeMax saw a real increase in employee satisfaction, and even suppliers' goodwill, generated by ADMB. The power of emotive bonding to create business value with consumers may be obvious, but the power to create incremental value with employees is equally compelling: new research from Gallup shows that employees who feel an emotional connection show increased discretionary effort.[18] At the heart of any social innovation is value creation: solving social problems in a way that creates enormous business value in the process.

Although Ronald McDonald House and OfficeMax's ADMB may appear to some to be typical corporate philanthropy, it is not the programs themselves that represent social innovation, but the powerful emotional bonds they produce using social impact. As companies seek to design emotive customer bonding initiatives, they should keep in mind that the key to success is producing meaningful social outcomes by leveraging the core business. ADMB does this. And although Ronald McDonald House may not exactly leverage the core business of McDonald's (hamburgers), the social impact created directly benefits families (most of whom are already

McDonald's customers) in such deep and meaningful ways that the customer bond still relates back to the business.

The *Backstory*: How We Got Here

Several key trends are driving the primacy of emotive customer bonding.

1. The Search for Meaning

Most everyone today is looking for something more than a paycheck—from the eighty-five million boomers entering retirement, to the fifty million Gen Xers struggling to balance work and family, to the seventy-six million Internet-raised Millennials. Especially the Millennials—social consciousness is just hardwired into their DNA. But they don't just want to merely do good; they want to solve world problems. In the words of one commentator: "Are you going to do something merely innovative—or something world-changingly awesome?"[19] The evidence is abundant: 61 percent of thirteen- to twenty-five-year-olds feel personally responsible for making a difference in the world; 81 percent have volunteered in the past year; 69 percent consider a company's social and environmental commitment when deciding where to shop; and 83 percent will trust a company more if it is socially or environmentally responsible.[20] And it's not just young dreamers: the Social Enterprise Club is now the largest club at Harvard Business School. Net Impact—a nonprofit whose mission is to inspire, educate, and equip individuals to use the power of business to create a more socially and environmentally sustainable world—has over fifteen thousand members around the world.

As you may recall from Chapter One, The Rise of the Social Capital Market, more and more of us are living the LOHAS way—lifestyles of health and sustainability, with a dramatically increased focus on personal development, sustainable living, the environment, and social justice. LOHAS comprises 63 million

U.S. consumers, with $227 billion in annual spend.[21] And many more than that number are looking for meaning, including showing partiality to companies that connect with their values.

2. Cause Commoditization

As discussed in Chapter Three, Corporate Social Innovation, it seems like everyone's giving to some cause, at both the personal and corporate levels. Just giving money to charity—or asking customers to do this on your behalf—doesn't cut it anymore. Some are even calling it "cause-washing."[22] The field has evolved to a greater level of sophistication, focusing on not just whether there's a connection to a social issue, but whether the connection makes sense for the company (say, a clear connection between social features and functional features).[23] But today, even logical "alignment" of company and cause isn't enough—it's just a necessary predicate to the real outcome of deep emotional engagement. To achieve it, companies must push beyond superficial alignment and tenuous connections (like donating ten cents to a nonprofit with every purchase or by clicking a Facebook ad) and find ways of actually *solving* social problems. According to Harvard Business School marketing professor V. Kasturi Rangan, "the most authentic brands going forward … will not only have to be transparent about how they are raising money and how they are spending it, they also now will have to show they are having a social impact … it is something that corporations that really want to differentiate themselves are going to have to step up for." Emotion is like a drug, and consumers have clearly built up a high level of resistance from overdosing on cheap cause hits.

3. The Blanding of Branding

Cause marketing isn't the only thing we see too much of today; we see too much of everything. A typical grocery store carries 61 varieties of sunscreen, 40 toothpaste options, 150 lipsticks, 230 soup offerings, 175 salad dressings (16 varieties of "Italian" alone),

275 choices of cereal, 22 types of frozen waffles, 85 brands of crackers, and 285 cookie varieties (and probably, in some holiday specialty store, multiple types of partridges in several different varieties of pear trees).[24]

Competition is infinite. A flat world and low barriers to entry, thanks especially to the Internet, have neutered the biggest product differentiators: price, quality, and convenience. These are now truly at parity. The result is a profusion of choices, especially in the retail channel. The implication is that companies need a new differentiator to connect their brands to the market, one that will deepen the loyalty of existing customers and provide a powerful, sustainable value proposition for new ones, something they can believe in and buy into. Daniel Pink, author of *A Whole New Mind*, wrote: "because of Abundance, businesses are realizing that the only way to differentiate their goods and services in today's overstocked marketplace is to make their offerings physically beautiful and emotionally compelling."[25]

Emotive customer bonding meets all three of these trends with a strategy that creates increased loyalty and brand value through an authentic, sustainable bond between customer and company.

The *Formula*: How to Make It Work

OfficeMax's ADMB did a number of things right that differentiated this strategy from simple philanthropy or cause marketing. Here's what it takes to make a successful emotive customer bonding strategy:

1. Own an Outcome

People value outcomes, not causes. Outcomes are changes in behavior, condition, or status that result from a social intervention or strategy. Education is an issue; eliminating the need for teachers to fund their own classroom supplies is an outcome, and one that OfficeMax could own. By raising the visibility of the issue and mobilizing their supplier base, the media, and their customers, they can make a real dent in the problem.

Too many companies try to own an issue or a cause—AIDS, health care, education, breast cancer, and so on. But an issue is just a big problem. And most issues are too broad for any one company to own or to make a real dent in. Moreover, customers and employees want to feel like they're making a difference in the world by improving real lives. That's where most efforts fall short.

Procter & Gamble learned this lesson quickly. When the company first launched its Pampers campaign in partnership with UNICEF, they hired a PR firm to conduct focus groups with their core constituents: moms. P&G explained the partnership with UNICEF, and the fact that maternal and newborn tetanus is a preventable disease, responsible for the deaths of one baby approximately every three minutes and up to thirty thousand mothers each year. Then the company announced that for every package of Pampers they bought, P&G would donate seven cents to UNICEF. Moms were nonplussed. So P&G decided to go back to the drawing board and convened a new focus group of moms, this time presenting a different proposition: *For every pack of Pampers you buy, Pampers will provide UNICEF with funding for one life-saving tetanus vaccine that will benefit a woman in need and her newborn in seventeen developing countries. By buying a pack of Pampers, you will save a life.* This time, the response from the focus group moms was overwhelming. People value outcomes, not issues. (Seven cents was, of course, the actual cost of one tetanus vaccine.) P&G also chose an outcome that is ownable and achievable. In fact, as of early 2010 P&G customers had already funded over fifty million life-saving vaccines in twenty-seven countries.[26] According to UNICEF estimates, 386 million vaccines are needed to wipe out tetanus in the forty-six countries that have yet to eliminate the disease,[27] and Pampers' global goal over the next three years is to provide funding for more than half of the needed (two hundred million) tetanus vaccines.[28] The strategy has paid off for P&G

by winning support (and higher in-store visibility) from retailers like Walmart, Target, and Tesco, which has led to incremental increases in sales of Pampers.[29]

2. Connect to Your Core

No company, no matter how big, can solve a social problem through marketing. You have to tap into the machinery of the core business. OfficeMax sells office supplies; that's what the company does. And suppliers of office supplies are also part of its core business. It was not only logical for OfficeMax to address the problem of teacher-funded classrooms—it was easy. Rather than donating money, or its customers' money, to an issue, OfficeMax mobilized the machinery of its business to help solve the problem. For ADMB, OfficeMax involved thousands of employees, from Ottawa to Illinois, including some from nonsales divisions: for example, individuals from accounts payable packed supply boxes. But the company went a step further by involving vendors—who donated many of the supplies given to teachers—and even employees' families. For example, one employee's brother donated all the label-makers given to the teachers.

OfficeMax figured out a way to use the platform of their business to create real social value—connecting supply with demand—in a way that benefited their business too. By using what you already do and what you know best, you can make the biggest impact.

3. Engage People in a Meaningful Way

At a local CVS pharmacy, the cashier asked if I wanted to add a dollar to my purchase to support St. Jude's Hospital. "Are *you* giving a dollar, or am *I* giving a dollar?" I asked. "You" was the reply. I left feeling even *less* respect for the brand, and somewhat taken advantage of (aren't they the ones making the profit on my purchase?).

Unfortunately, that's typical of most run-of-the-mill cause marketing campaigns these days: the simple act of a company donating a few cents of their profits—or even worse, someone else's money—to a large charity does not create a bond or any social value. It's just reshuffling money. An emotional connection is something that must be *earned*. The most effective strategies are authentic; they often involve taking action in a meaningful way other than simply contributing money. OfficeMax tacked no purchase requirement onto ADMB and didn't require schools to commit to buying anything in the future. And the OfficeMax employees who participated actually hand-delivered the supplies into classrooms and participated in the emotional experience. That stuck with them forever: remember, 99 percent said ADMB made them feel proud to work for OfficeMax.

4. Let Others Tell Your Story

It's often said that the best way to impress is to let others brag about you. Moms are great for that. So rather than take out flashy ads or issue press releases, Pampers let moms spread the word. P&G convened a "Pampers Mommy Blogger Event" to educate web-savvy moms about the campaign. One mommy blogger (named Alphamom) wrote: "As mothers, it is our instinct to help those we see in harm's way ... After watching this footage of Bryan McCleary (director of external relations for P&G baby care) in Angola, there was not a dry eye in the room or a blogger who wasn't committed to making a difference."[30]

Moms were equipped with materials to help spread the word—and an online donation button to add to their sites. Although Alphamom did her part, P&G's partner, UNICEF, enlisted the help of *übermom* actress Salma Hayek to advocate for the cause. OfficeMax also used maternal power with recent incarnations of ADMB: in 2009, the company invited thirty-two influential women in social media, or Max Moms, to help create awareness of the underfunded classrooms issue. Max Moms wrote 120 blog posts on the topic, helped fuel over seven thousand Twitter tweets about the cause, and hosted events in thirty-two cities to gather supplies for local teachers; their efforts helped secure a total of eleven million audience impressions![31] But online is just one venue. ADMB also transformed employees, teachers, students and their parents, and celebrity volunteers into powerful word-of-mouth ambassadors.

5. Create a Wraparound

It's not just about an event, or a promotion. Emotive customer bonding is about immersing customers, employees, and others in a 360-degree brand experience that reinforces social impact on many levels. HSBC Holdings is a case in point. The global financial services powerhouse was the first of the big banks to go "carbon neutral" back in 2005, winning the bank many accolades.[32] To extend this strategy, HSBC has also pioneered a suite of new consumer financial products and services focused on sustainable businesses, including environmental liability insurance, climate risk consulting, consumer insurance products linked to forest protection and clean air initiatives in certain countries, microfinance loans, and rural banking initiatives in China.[33] HSBC wraps its philanthropy around these business strategies, allocating 75 percent of its $102-million community investment strategy to environmental and educational themes.[34] Finally, HSBC has made climate change one of three dominant issues to be included in the bank's lending policies.[35] This comprehensive wraparound deepens the customer's emotional bond with the business and reinforces the authenticity of the bank's commitment to climate change.

Emotive bonding doesn't have to cost a lot of money. In fact, OfficeMax had a tiny budget and spent virtually nothing on promotion or marketing for ADMB. But this strategy, like all other social innovations, relies on finding new and creative ways to mobilize the platform of the business to solve important social problems.

The *Pitfalls*: What to Watch Out For

While it's easy to associate your brand with a good cause, it's tough to meet the higher threshold of emotional connection. Here are some tips to avoid getting lost in the chasm between cause marketing and emotive customer bonding.

1. Don't Proceed Without Executive Buy-In

Great ideas for emotive bonding strategies can come from anywhere in the organization, but because they are so integral to the business itself, they must have the full and visible support of leadership. OfficeMax used multiple pilots, including a five-site single-day version for the ADMB program, to work out execution-related kinks but primarily to sell senior execs on the idea. It's also important for the business leaders to fully accept that this is a business proposition and not just philanthropy. Short of that, you'll never get access to the key levers of the business (operations, suppliers, marketing, and so on) that are so essential to making this strategy effective.

2. Don't Guess

The companies that do this well do their homework. You can't bond with a customer you don't know. Who are you trying to reach, to affect? What problems matter most to them? OfficeMax put a lot of effort into identifying prototypical customer Eve and laying out her needs, interests, and what she would value most, in terms of products, in-store experience, and branding. But this takes more than just market research. It requires researching the social issues that make the most sense for your company to solve and how specifically you can address the problem. OfficeMax went beyond "education" to get to the problem of teacher-funded classrooms, which intersected with their locus of impact and their customers' passions. P&G went beyond "children's charity" to laser focus in on a problem for which they could uniquely make a difference.

3. Don't Confuse This with Cause Marketing

Emotive bonding is not about a short-lived promotion, tacking on a few extra cents for a good cause, or even partnering with a charity. It's about leveraging the core business to solve social problems in ways that create a deep, meaningful, and enduring connection with customers. In the Pampers example, moms cared about saving lives. In the words of one mommy blogger: "I love this because it is easy and simple to understand and ultimately connects moms in the developed world who want to help moms in the developing world."[36]

4. Business-to-Business (B2B) Has Emotion, Too

Emotive customer bonding can also work as a way for businesses to make connections not just with consumers but with other companies and within themselves. Companies are made of people, and people can be bonded. Take McDonald's. The company, through Ronald McDonald House Charities, bonds with other companies, including key partners like Southwest Airlines, which adopted RMHC as its primary corporate charity. Southwest employees coast to coast regularly volunteer at the Ronald McDonald houses, and twice a year the airline sponsors dinners at houses in every city Southwest serves. Southwest even dedicated a signature aircraft, "The Spirit of Hope," in honor of the thirtieth birthday of the first Ronald McDonald House. In this way, Southwest is creating a lasting bond with the McDonald's brand through leveraging the Ronald McDonald House program to build emotional bonds with its own employees and customers around the country.

The power of emotive customer bonding, and the logic behind its innovation, lies in creating a more human and authentic relationship between a large, faceless company and its employees, customers, and business partners. In today's hyper-competitive, undifferentiated marketplace, keeping existing customers is just as difficult as acquiring new ones. And the beauty of this, for social change advocates, is that the best way to achieve these business results is for companies to create meaningful social impact.

Chapter 7

STRATEGY FOUR: DEVELOP NEW PIPELINES FOR TALENT

Talent has never been harder to find. And it's not because there's a labor shortage (in fact, unemployment rates are now at a sixteen-year high). Rather, companies are talent-starved because the pace of business is changing more rapidly than the pace of education. Fewer people have the specific skills companies are looking for, even in entry-level positions. That's where the next social innovation comes in: pipelining talent. As we'll see, the U.S. education system is failing to produce job-ready students. Rather than bemoaning the situation, more and more companies are taking action, creating alternative education pathways that will better prepare young (and not-so-young) people for jobs in their industries. These new pipelines result in valuable career opportunities for the community and a more effective workforce for the company.

High School, Inc.: Travelers' Hartford Insurance and Finance Academy

Travelers Insurance isn't a company that gives up easily. With $110 billion in assets and about $25 billion of annual revenues, the insurance company can afford pretty much anything it wants.

But Travelers almost gave up on Hartford, the city where it was founded—or at least on Hartford's public schools. In recent years the insurer, through its foundation, had invested hundreds of thousands of dollars into dozens of nonprofits that aimed to improve the Hartford Public School system with supplemental education programs and other efforts. But Hartford students' grades kept declining. In fact, they performed so poorly that even within the group of lowest-scoring school districts in Connecticut, Hartford was well below average.[1] Perhaps this was no surprise for a city considered America's second poorest, despite its location in the country's second wealthiest state; the gap between the academic performance of Connecticut's poor and non-poor students was the widest of any U.S. state.[2]

According to the CEO of the Travelers Foundation, Marlene Ibsen, employees associated with the school initiatives were disheartened, and cynicism about whether anything could be done to help the school system was pervasive throughout the city of Hartford.[3] Travelers felt a growing frustration and wrestled with whether continuing to give money as they had been was going to make any difference at all. Then they met new Hartford Public School superintendent Steven Adamowski. Adamowski, who took over the superintendent position in late 2006, came to Hartford with thirty-five years of experience as an educator and school reformer; he also held a doctorate. More importantly, he had a track record: from 1998 to 2002, he had turned around Cincinnati Public Schools, using a comprehensive program—including a thoughtful accountability system, budgeting, and alignment of teacher evaluation and compensation—that had gained national attention.[4] Most important to Travelers managers, Adamowski spoke a language they understood: "His approach made sense to us as businesspeople," the foundation CEO said. Rather than any quick fixes, Adamowski laid out a twelve-year plan. He noted that as a whole, Connecticut's school system was improving about 1 percent annually on academic measures, and that Harford would have to improve at four times that rate just to catch up. He also acknowledged the city's dismal high school graduation rate: 29 percent.[5]

So what was Adamowski's plan and how did Travelers fit into it? A key element of the plan was a "school choice model"—themed programs that offered more personalized learning environments. In this context, Adamowski wanted Travelers to run a high school on the company's campus, allowing students to learn in the classrooms and apply what they learned in Travelers' offices. While Travelers liked the idea of exposing high schoolers to insurance industry concepts and opportunities, they were reluctant to take responsibility for an entire school. Instead, they suggested starting an insurance and financial services academy that could be supported by multiple companies in the area. This would both prevent the school district from placing all its eggs in the Travelers basket and allow Travelers to share program expenses with peers—in part because Travelers knew that not every participant in the program would ultimately work for them.

Travelers discussed the idea with Adamowski in 2007, and the new high school program was a prominent element of a $1 million commitment to support the Hartford Public Schools reform plan to the following year. The size of the grant meant discontinuing grants for several other grantees, but Travelers believed the deeper benefits of a more focused, intensive approach to education would offset these cuts. Travelers' early and aggressive stance also gave peer companies confidence to join the effort, as well as other parts of the reform. Specific supporters of the academy included Wachovia, Webster Bank, and The Hartford. They worked in partnership with the National Academy Foundation (NAF), a network of five hundred high school career academies based mostly in urban areas.

High School, Inc., the insurance and finance academy that emerged from the initiative, was scheduled to open in the fall of 2009, as part of Hartford's new "all-choice" system, which allowed soon-to-be high school freshmen and sophomores to choose the academy that fit their aspirations best. Among their choices were schools specializing in nursing, journalism, and green technology—about a dozen institutions in all. High School, Inc., was designed as an independent college preparatory school that could accommodate four hundred high school students (grades nine through twelve) who were interested in insurance and other financial services careers. The industry-vetted curriculum was based on the NAF finance model, which would expose students to multiple elements of insurance and finance-related careers while still providing basic English, math, science, and social studies courses. Specific academy themes included insurance (including health insurance), banking, investments/securities, international business, and financial services. More broadly, students would undertake a planned sequence of specialized courses and gain real-world experience applying what they learned through internships (seventy paid ones were available), interactions with mentors, brown bag lunches, job shadowing, tutoring, and field work programs.[6]

A good part of the companies' enthusiasm for the program was based on its potential business benefits, specifically talent recruitment. In 2006, before the economic downturn that started in 2008, talent was hard to come by; according to some estimates, as much as 80 percent of the future workforce was going to have to come from urban centers. As the Travelers foundation CEO said, "We wanted to raise the urban students' awareness and preparedness levels before they went off to college. Most of them probably didn't grow up thinking, 'Someday I want to work for an insurance company.'" At the same time, students enrolling in the insurance academy would have chosen it from among the other themed schools, so they already had a basic interest in the field. And Hartford, considered the "insurance capital of the world," was a logical place to establish an insurance and finance academy.[7]

Through the program, Travelers hoped to identify high-potential students and get them excited about insurance industry opportunities so that they would consider such positions— including leadership roles down the road—with Travelers or other insurers. The academy, while teaching valuable skills, would thus be a pipeline for strong new talent. "We view it as a down payment in our potential future workforce," said Michael Klein, president of Travelers' commercial accounts and cochair of the academy's advisory board.[8]

Of course, students gained major benefits from the program, as well. These included the beginnings of a valuable career network. As Terrell Hill, High School, Inc.'s principal noted, "In business, it's not always what you know, but who you know. Many of these kids don't have those types of connections."[9] Beyond career-related advantages, the new program gave its students much better odds of making academic progress: NAF-based academies in general had a 90-percent graduation rate, with over 80 percent of graduates moving on to college.[10]

The *Innovation*: Why This Strategy Works

Pipelining talent is about businesses taking ownership of the education problem in this country (of part of it, at least) and developing alternative pathways to prepare students for future employment. Simply put, schools aren't delivering on the skills and training needed for today's workforce, and companies don't have time to wait (or hope) for public education to catch up. So to keep pace with increasing economic demands for specialization, companies are helping students bypass the standard public education system while grooming them for industry-specific careers.

These next-generation education strategies are designed, managed, and funded by companies with the purpose of directly pipelining students into a particular company or industry. Take IBM. Working with multiple universities to identify the types of skills graduates would need to compete in the fast-changing global economy (and specifically at IBM), the company developed an entirely new academic discipline called Service Science, Management and Engineering (SSME); SSME combines computer science, engineering, management sciences, and business strategies—areas that are generally separate in traditional higher education. Students can even obtain a certificate in SSME from such prestigious institutions as the University of California, Berkeley. Today, SSME-based courses are available through over 250 institutions representing fifty countries—among these are Italy, Vietnam, South Africa, and Australia.[11] For IBM this is not a philanthropic initiative, but a core business strategy. The company says it invests $100 million a year in its university initiatives; funding for its SSME efforts, which are part of that, have increased 30 percent in the past three years.[12] The firm's motivation is to both help students and help themselves: IBM and other tech firms like Xerox are hungry for graduates with the skills SSME emphasizes.[13] A *Wall Street Journal* headline in 2006 summed it up nicely: "Majoring in IBM: Dissatisfied with Graduates, Companies Design and Fund Curricula at Universities."[14]

Thus, across business sectors, support for education is evolving from a philanthropic passion to a business priority. Concomitantly, companies are evolving their education strategies—from philanthropy to social innovation. In 2007 alone, businesses donated more than $2 billion to education,[15] with precious little to show for it. Companies can't afford to take any more chances. Pipelining talent is a business strategy to more efficiently train, develop, and absorb the talent that companies desperately need in order to grow and compete. And companies are pipelining talent in a number of innovative ways, from specialized academies to college curricula to apprenticeships and even virtual classrooms.

The *Backstory*: How We Got Here

Workforce magazine calls it "Business Goes to Kindergarten." In an article titled "Fast Forward: 25 Trends That Will Change the Way You Do Business," *Workforce* stated:

> All signs indicate that corporate involvement in public schools—already redefining kindergarten-through-high-school education—will continue to increase over the next

decade. Alarmed by under-performing public schools and students poorly equipped for the job market, business is getting directly involved.

Corporate sponsors are popping up on campuses from Washington, D.C., to Stockton, California, as a new generation of students prepares for college, and for jobs such as auto mechanics, Internet specialists, and hotel workers. School-to-business field trips start in kindergarten. Internships, meetings with top executives in office settings, and even paychecks are available for older students.[16]

Why is this happening? What is the direct economic interest of corporations, if any, in American public education? Three drivers have led companies to develop social innovation strategies around education: (1) the failure of the public education system to deliver job-ready talent, (2) frustration with globalization, and (3) the rise of middle-skills jobs.

1. Failure of Public Education to Produce Job-Ready Talent

"Most corporations today don't trust America's education system to produce workers with the skills they need."[17] That's a quote from a public school official—unfortunately, it's a very apt assessment.

We're all familiar with the disconcerting public education statistics: the high school dropout rate still hovers near 10 percent nationwide[18]; by fourth grade, Black and Latino students are nearly three years behind their white peers[19]; only 9 percent of young adults from low-income families graduate from college by age twenty-four[20]; and the costs of public education are still on the rise, estimated as of this writing at $543 billion for K–12 education in the United States.[21] Equally startling is the yawning global achievement gap between America and almost every other Organisation for Economic Co-operation and Development (OECD) nation: the United States ranked twenty-fifth out of thirty in math and twenty-fourth in science, putting our average youth on par with those from Portugal and the Slovak Republic.[22] But ultimately those are more public policy concerns than business issues. What businesses care about is simple: can they get the talent they need? The answer, at least from U.S. public education, is no.

So the deficiencies in American public education are not just about academic achievement. They're also about work readiness. Somehow "vocational" education has become a pejorative term, reminiscent of carving wooden doorstops in high school shop classes. Our schools have drawn a false dichotomy between "college" and "vocational" training, and in the process they have lost a huge opportunity to integrate practical workforce skills into the mainstream academic curriculum. So we now have two tracks of students: those that are college-ready but not job-ready, and those that are neither job-ready nor college-ready. In both cases, schools are not preparing students to enter the workforce, whether straight from high school or even after college. In our zealous desire to promote "college for all," we may have overcorrected: focusing everyone on achieving the dream of college while failing to develop more robust vocational programs and alternative career pathways. The truth is, not everyone is going to Yale—and not everyone *wants* to go to Yale (no offense, Bulldogs). Unfortunately, a lot of kids get shoehorned into going to *some* college, only to drop out later.

Net result: a lot of talent falls through the cracks.

But even if 100 percent of students were to graduate from high school, the *type* of skills that corporations require today is very different than the skills most schools are teaching. The need for these new skills has emerged from a dramatic shift in our economy: from manufacturing jobs to service sector jobs. Between 1995 and 2005, three million manufacturing jobs were lost, while seventeen million service sector jobs were created.[23] Companies are now operating in an era of "twenty-first-century skills"—advanced critical-thinking skills that allow workers to analyze complex problems, consider data, and work in teams to generate solutions. But the problem is that our schools are out of synch. Tony Wagner, author of *The Global Achievement Gap*, wrote, "our system of public education—our curricula, teaching methods, and the tests we require students to take—were created in a different century for the needs of another era."[24] He cites the seven survival skills that companies are looking for today:

- Critical thinking and problem-solving

- Collaboration across networks and leading by influence

- Agility and adaptability

- Initiative and entrepreneurialism

- Effective oral and written communication

- Accessing and analyzing information

- Curiosity and imagination[25]

Not exactly the stuff we learned in eighth-grade social studies.

In his book *A Whole New Mind*, Daniel Pink talks about the skills required to succeed in today's economy in a slightly different way. He argues we've moved from an information age that values knowledge workers with "logical, linear, computer-like capabilities" to a conceptual age that values right-brain thinkers with "inventive, empathic, big-picture capabilities."[26] Thus Pink's twenty-first-century skills fall into two categories: "high concept" capabilities that include the ability to create artistic and emotional beauty, to detect patterns and opportunities, to craft a satisfying narrative, and to combine seemingly unrelated ideas into a novel invention; and "high touch" skills that involve the ability to empathize, to understand the subtleties of human interaction, to find joy in one's self and to elicit it in others, and to stretch beyond the quotidian, in pursuit of purpose and meaning. The need for high concept and high touch is on the rise worldwide, in the global economy and society in general.

This deepening corporate thirst for talent—combined with the inability of public schools to produce this talent—drives companies to create *their own* business strategies for social change, in the form of educational programs that foster the right kind of talent.

2. Globalization Is No Panacea

So if American schools can't keep up with those of other countries, why don't companies just hire the talent they need from abroad? After all, China produces approximately 950,000 engineers *per year* (compared to our 60,000), and has roughly 8.5 million young professional graduates with up to seven years' work experience each. Another ninety-seven million trained students are waiting in the wings.[27] America imports most of its oil from Canada, Mexico, and Nigeria, so why not import our engineers and workers from China and India?

Turns out globalization isn't quite the labor panacea everyone thought.

Globalization seems to work well enough for commoditized functions: manufacturing, programming, and mechanical, repeatable processes like customer service inquiries (like all those India-based call centers) and even X-ray analysis. But in a service-oriented economy that increasingly values twenty-first-century skills like teamwork, collaboration, and effective communication, and "inventive, empathic, big-picture capabilities"—to quote Pink—global labor searches are becoming less effective. A recent McKinsey study noted that for U.S.-based corporations trying to recruit foreign professionals, "poor English skills, dubious educational qualifications, and cultural issues—such as a lack of experience on teams and a reluctance to take initiative or assume leadership roles—were among the problems most frequently cited."[28] Moreover, despite the seemingly infinite stream of highly educated young workers, multinational companies are finding that few graduates have the necessary skills for service occupations. Take Chinese engineers, for example. While China produces nearly one million engineers per year, these students are trained in a highly theoretical fashion, typically with very little practical experience in projects or teamwork, making it difficult for them to transition from academia to a fast-paced workplace.

And there's yet another reason why globalization can't sate corporate appetites: emerging economies, many for the first time, are growing at such a rate that they are now absorbing their own talent, leaving suboptimal resources for American firms and multinationals. It's what people are calling a "reverse brain drain" in the United States. Not only are we having a tougher time recruiting foreign nationals to come work in the United States, but many of those that are already here—whether for education or career—are choosing to leave. According to reports with titles like "Losing the World's Best and Brightest" (a joint effort of Harvard, Duke, and UC Berkeley), increasing numbers of foreign students graduating from U.S. schools with science and engineering degrees are leaving for opportunities back at home. For example, India is experiencing a "brain gain" that started several years ago; in 2007, over forty thousand Indian IT workers returned from the United States and the UK to work in Bangalore. Other trends suggest a "brain retain" for countries like India and China: until 2001, 35 percent of graduates from India's prestigious Indian Institutes of Technology (IITs) moved abroad; as of 2002 that figure had dropped to 16 percent, and today only 17 percent of recent IIT grads see the United States as holding the most promising career opportunities, whereas 72 percent say it's India.[29]

3. The Importance of "Middle-Skills" Jobs

Nearly half (about 45 percent) of all jobs created between 2004 and 2014 will be "middle-skills" jobs—those that require more than a high school diploma but less than a college degree.[30] Much has been made about America's shortage of highly skilled workers, but less is known about the availability of middle-skill professionals such as plumbers, electricians, health care workers, legal assistants, machinists, and police officers—demand for such employees is expected to continue despite the economic downturn.[31] For example, health care jobs requiring less than a college degree are expected to grow from 20 to 40 percent, adding more than 1.5 million job openings.[32] Similarly, employment in the skilled construction trades (such as carpenters, bricklayers, plumbers) is expected to grow by 10 to 15 percent and provide 4.6 million jobs.[33]

All of these jobs still require specialized skills and education beyond a high school diploma, providing a strong incentive to expand the number of "alternative educational pathways." These pathways include career academies (like Hartford's Finance and Insurance Academy); tech prep and other high-quality vocational training in secondary school (the preferred term is now "career and technical education," and it involves much more in-depth training; students learning automotive skills study computer diagnostics and hydrogen fuel cells[34]); the nation's 1,655 community colleges (which, at an average annual tuition of $1,416, offer a compelling value); and web-based learning platforms (the University of Phoenix Online Campus now has the number-one enrollment among all colleges or universities, boasting 165,373 students).[35]

Private-sector apprenticeships are also coming back into vogue, serving as a powerful antidote to high-school dropout rates. *Time* magazine noted, "It may be hard for Americans to fathom a world in which corporations, instead of merely lamenting the shortage of skilled labor, volunteer to train vast numbers of the non-college-bound. Oh, yeah, and to pay them a bundle along the way."[36] Many are looking to Germany's success with its "earn-while-you-learn" system. Under this system, German corporations are paying 1.6 million young adults to train for about 350 types of jobs, ranging from industrial mechanic to baker to fitness trainer.[37] The trainees' average annual salary of $19,913 helps explain why less than 9 percent of Germans drop out of high school: they can't get in on the action without a diploma.[38] In fact, 58 percent of students finished high school holding three-year training contracts, and more than two-thirds of this group secure permanent positions during the contract period. Also, despite increasing pressure from globalization and a shrinking labor market at home, 23 percent of all German companies continue to offer apprenticeships. This way of training the future workforce is beginning to take hold in America: there are nearly half a million American workers in the registered apprenticeship system and at least another half a million are in other apprenticeship programs.[39]

These alternative pathways present ready opportunities for social innovation, as they offer convenient platforms for specialized training and serve as direct feeders into the workforce.

The *Formula*: How This Strategy Works

To create the right kind of talent pipelines, you have to start by identifying the right outcomes and using those to make a clear business case for your involvement in education. Specifically, what social and business outcomes are you trying to accomplish? Once the answer is clear, and bought into, the strategy will be more successful. At the same time, there is no one set way to pipeline talent. Every company brings a different set of needs, a different culture, and a different set of capabilities to the table. But all aspiring talent pipeliners must stay focused on the nexus between positive educational outcomes and business value. As long as you are maximizing both, *using your core business capabilities*, you are engaging in social innovation.

1. Build the Business Case

First things first: whatever you do must make sense for the business. Over the years, corporations have developed a steady stream of "signature" education programs, many becoming the CEO's pride and joy. These programs are designed to stimulate everything from interest in robotics to afterschool sports. But as companies start to realize the business implications of an underdeveloped workforce, the opportunity cost of feel-good corporate education initiatives becomes glaringly obvious: these resources could be better spent producing education outcomes that directly benefit the business.

Remember, social innovation isn't merely about *aligning* with your company's core business strategy; it's about *driving* your company's core business strategy. To do that, you need to be clear about your biggest priorities. Take Travelers, for instance. One of the insurer's biggest business priorities was to tap into the high-growth minority insurance market. According to the Census Bureau, minority groups now represent over ninety-eight million people in the United States, more than one third of the entire population. But selling into that market is tricky. According to Don Davis, of Travelers Emerging Markets, "We're dependent on agents who know the culture, know the language and know the buying habits of the minority consumers they are trying to capture."[40] The problem is, Travelers doesn't have enough minority agents. And industry-wide, African-Americans constitute only 0.8 percent of agency principals; Asian-Americans tally 1.3 percent; and Latinos, 1.8 percent.[41]

High School, Inc.—the Hartford Finance and Insurance Academy—links clearly to a broader Travelers strategy called "Travelers EDGE: Empowering Dreams for Education and Employment," a social innovation program to pipeline high-potential talent from traditionally underserved populations into the business. Growing diversity at Travelers directly advances a priority business objective for the company: servicing high-growth minority markets. And it's a business objective that likely wouldn't be achieved without the talent pipeline offered by High School, Inc.

The bottom line for business is that it's still about the bottom line and always will be. The big "Aha!" about social innovation is that if you can hook directly into a company's business engine, the resources, level of commitment, and ultimately social impact will be much greater than when you're running on the fumes of goodwill.

But the business case for pipelining talent needn't always hinge on recruiting needs; sometimes the talent flows the other way—from the business to the community. IBM developed an innovative "reverse-flow" pipeline to transition its older employees into second careers. Called Transition to Teaching, the initiative helps interested employees find opportunities as K–12 math and science teachers in classrooms around the nation, to address the critical shortage of qualified instructors. IBM also developed a Transitions to Government program that works with the Partnership for Public Service and various federal agencies to "create a corporate transition program that identifies, recruits, and successfully hires interested IBM employees and retirees for key jobs in the federal government."[42] In both cases, the company is making a positive social impact while reducing the costs associated with transitioning workers through more traditional means—layoffs, expensive early retirement packages, and the like.

2. Leverage Your Core Competency

What's different about social innovation from other socially focused efforts is that it's about using your *core business* to solve social problems in ways that are financially beneficial. Some companies have interpreted the notion of "leveraging the business" rather loosely. Lending employees to a local nonprofit to help with the organization's branding and website may be a worthy effort, but it's not social innovation. In the case of Travelers, their core business involves hiring insurance agents to sell insurance. By pipelining future talent, Travelers "aimed" their business at a relevant social problem (creating jobs for disadvantaged youth) and did it in a way that directly advances the goals of the business (recruiting minority agents).

Cisco Networking Academy is another example of leveraging a core competency. The company realized that demand for the Internet (Cisco's core product is routers) was outpacing the supply of trained information technology specialists available to support it. The issue was so severe that it threatened the company's ability to grow. So Cisco created a Networking Academy to train economically disadvantaged youth and women in networking and information technology (IT) skills, ultimately becoming Cisco-certified technicians. The program has been a huge hit: to date, Cisco has trained more than 2.75 million students in 165 different countries, from Afghanistan to Zimbabwe. Ninety-one percent of those students use the skills they have learned on a daily basis; 79 percent pursue more education in IT; and 29 percent have started a business in IT. This is an extraordinary social impact, and it's also advancing Cisco's core business of supporting and selling its products. That's social innovation.

3. Choose the Right Pipeline

The real innovation in pipelining talent is not about "fixing" the education system; rather, it's about creating alternate pathways for getting students into the workforce. Be careful not to take a one-size-fits-all approach. Based on your company's business objectives, determine the model that works best—from academies to apprenticeships, and everything in between.

For Cisco, whose core business involves networking technologies, choosing the right model was a no-brainer: virtual training via online courses and interactive tools. Cisco created a network of over nine thousand academies through partnerships with public and private institutions including schools, universities, businesses, nonprofits, and government organizations. These partners help to develop and deliver course content, improve the effectiveness and accessibility of the program, increase access to education and career opportunities, and ensure that students and instructors have the resources necessary to accomplish their goals. Cisco also partners with government agencies, businesses, nonprofits, and international NGOs to support its students and alumni in their educational, entrepreneurial, and occupational endeavors.

Unlike Cisco, Travelers had to work through several models before they got it right. Recall that the Hartford Public Schools superintendent first asked Travelers to run a high school on their corporate campus, with hundreds of students coming in and out of their offices every day! Travelers liked the idea of getting more involved in education but didn't want full responsibility for running a school. Eventually, Travelers signed on to the Finance and Insurance Academy model through a partnership with several other financial service firms. Given the likelihood that Travelers would not be the only firm hiring these students, it made sense to develop a nonexclusive pipeline to share costs and broaden the appeal of the academy.

Beyond your core business objectives, there are four criteria to consider in choosing the right kind of pipeline:

- *Involvement.* Do you want to design and run a school, develop a curriculum, or partner with an existing provider?

- *Investment.* What resources make sense for your company to invest in this type of strategy? For Travelers, it started with a $1 million commitment. Cisco has invested over $150 million since 1997. IBM spends $100 million a year on pipelining strategies!

- *Outcomes.* Are you looking to hire students directly, stimulate interest in a particular field, disseminate knowledge, build affinity in future customers, or some combination of these?

- *Community.* Are you focused locally or globally? What are the needs of the community or population you are trying to serve? Where can you add the most value?

4. Demonstrate ROI

Being able to measure the direct contribution to your business is always critical, but especially with strategies that are potentially more indirect, like education. If you want the company to view efforts in this area as a business strategy, it's critical that you speak the language of business. Travelers developed an elaborate measurement system to track EDGE's business impact. Among the items measured were number of positions filled, ROI/cost per position filled, changes in employee attitudes toward diversity, Travelers brand reputation among career counselors, impact on business partners (such as insurance brokers), and the company's visibility among key influencers. The company also has a specific pipeline measure that shows how many diverse candidates are interested, eligible, and pursuing a career in the insurance and financial services industry.

Most senior executives have been conditioned to look at corporate involvement in education as a philanthropic "nice to do" activity. There's nothing wrong with that. But the success of these initiatives ultimately depends on their being viewed as business strategies with a clear and direct ROI. Today's social innovators need to work hard to overcome legacy expectations about this work, and providing hard data tied to key business objectives is the best way to do that. Don't forget: philanthropic strategies get funded out of leftover profits; business strategies get funded out of operating budgets.

5. Get to Scale Quickly

The best way to ensure ROI is to get your strategy to scale. Fast. Not only does scale lead to greater impact, but it also allows you to amortize or spread your initial upfront investment over a larger set of results. Scale can also mean breadth. For example, Cisco found a way to extend its Networking Academy platform to address the country's health care challenges. The company partnered with Florida Community College at Jacksonville to integrate Cisco Networking Academy training into its Biomedical Engineering Technology degree program. Today, about 1,800 students per year participate in the academy program, learning how to install, inspect, and repair multiple types of equipment used in a range of health care settings. According to the college's director of academic systems, "when the biomedical technology program started, the students only took electronics and biomedical equipment courses. But now, almost all the equipment is connected to a network … If you think of networking as core technology, health care and other industries are moving closer to the core skill sets that Networking Academy courses provide."[43] Thus one key to scale is leveraging the right partners. The only way Travelers was able to get its Finance and Insurance Academy up and running was by partnering with the National Academy Foundation. And the only way that IBM was able to get its SSME curricula in front of enough students was by partnering with educators. There is a ready supply of school networks, nonprofits, and particularly community colleges that would be eager and valuable partners in pipelining arrangements. Seek them out.

The *Pitfalls*: What to Watch Out For

Although pipelining talent seems fairly straightforward, there are a number of ways companies can lapse back into a philanthropic mind-set and undermine the business case for this strategy. Here are some of the common pitfalls:

1. Don't Conflate Pipelining with Philanthropy

It's easy to get sidetracked by the larger social issue of solving America's education problem, but that's probably not in your job description. The way your company will make the biggest social impact is by focusing on the biggest business value. So when it comes to the issue of education, don't try to boil the ocean. Stay focused on results that matter to your business.

2. Don't Craft a Fifteen-Year Plan

Many education advocates are fond of saying that fixing the current system is a complex problem, and that companies must be patient and take the long view. Some insiders complain that their CEOs "just don't get it." But they do. Companies don't think in fifteen-year cycles, they think in quarters and years. Therefore you need to design strategies to produce results within this time frame. Leave it to foundations, governments, think tanks, and yes, educators, to worry about the long term, because that's truly their mission. Even as Travelers supported Hartford's long-term turnaround strategy, the company relies on its EDGE program to pipeline interns and hire "high-potential" employees on an annual basis.

Focus on the social problems that *make sense* for your business to solve, and solve them in the near term.

3. Don't Fall in Love with Your Partners

Partners are great, whether they be schools, nonprofits, or government agencies. But the partner isn't what matters; the outcomes are. Travelers partners with community colleges in Hartford, Baltimore, and St. Paul. The company measures each partner against key performance criteria and evaluates whether they're producing reasonable results, given the level of support and the time frame. Those who don't perform won't last. So don't fall in love with partners; fall in love with outcomes. Remember, you are investing in results, not just good causes.

Education is ripe for social innovation. The increasing number of corporations that face talent shortfalls must make a choice: wait for the education system to catch up, or build alternative education pathways to generate the talent necessary to compete. As the realities of outsourcing and globalization set in, and the requirement for specialized skills continues to grow, companies are realizing that education must be viewed first as a business strategy and second as a social issue.

Chapter 8

STRATEGY FIVE: INFLUENCE POLICY THROUGH REVERSE LOBBYING

The relationship between business and government has long been that of the regulated and the regulator, the favor-asker and the favor-granter. But that's changing quickly. Companies are increasingly working with governments to solve social problems and, in doing so, generating valuable business benefits. The strategy of backdoor market entry included public-private partnerships that help businesses enter hard-to-reach markets. In this chapter we discuss how corporations are offering their help to advance specific policy priorities that serve both public *and* corporate interests.

Why Safeway Is Lobbying for Universal Health Care

With all the talk about health care in the United States today, it's not surprising to see yet another group promoting universal coverage. But what's surprising about this particular group—the Coalition to Advance Healthcare Reform (CAHR)—is its membership: a who's who of the nation's largest corporations, over sixty companies in total, including General Mills, GlaxoSmithKline,

Wrigley, Kimberly-Clark, Aetna, PepsiCo, and Safeway. Safeway's role in the coalition has been especially important because the group was founded by Safeway CEO Steve Burd. And for many, including Safeway employees and Washington insiders, Burd is the last executive they'd expect to see clamoring for universal health care. In 2005, Burd had helped fellow California grocers force labor unions to accept stripped-down insurance packages. The reduced benefits saved the companies a lot of money, of course, but also prompted employee walk-outs that, in turn, led to news coverage of checkout clerks losing their homes and cars, and union management dubbing Burd "evil" and "a rat."[1]

Just two years later, Burd stood beside far-left Oregon Senator Ron Wyden on Capitol Hill to present the first universal-coverage proposal after Democrats regained control of the Senate. "Working together," Burd said in Washington, "business, labor, government, consumer groups, and health-care providers can collectively solve this problem."[2] These weren't empty words: Burd had collaborated with Wyden for a year to help draft the proposal. And CAHR, the group the CEO founded, has the explicit mission of advancing "solutions that reverse rising healthcare costs, solve the problem of the uninsured, and dramatically improve the quality of care for every American."[3]

In May 2007, CAHR launched a political campaign proposing extension of medical insurance to everyone, based partly on Governor Arnold Schwarzenegger's health care proposals for California; in fact, Schwarzenegger had incorporated several key elements of Safeway's health care plan—including incentives for preventive care—into his proposal.[4] The broad CAHR plan, which was to be pitched hard to legislators (including Republicans staunchly opposed to universal coverage), included required insurance for everyone, subsidized insurance for low-income segments, coverage of preexisting conditions, and incentives for healthy behavior.

So why Burd's sudden change of heart? Ostensibly there are three reasons: individuals' physical health, the nation's economic health, and Safeway's financial health. Universal coverage would theoretically improve citizens' health nationwide and, depending on the type of plan, potentially lead to healthier lifestyles, rather than just providing for treatment. Burd himself is a major fitness advocate, a sixty-year-old known for hitting the treadmill daily, lifting weights regularly, and watching his diet, along with captaining Safeway's softball team.[5] In the late 1990s he'd begun promoting healthy living to employees through newsletters and speeches, along with introducing screening and counseling for chronic diseases.[6] As will be discussed shortly in more detail, Safeway already rewards employees for healthy behavior. So Burd was happy to see that Wyden's legislation promoted healthy behavior, including providing incentives for employers to establish wellness programs and insurance discounts for employees enrolling in these.[7]

Burd's advocacy of universal coverage has also been aimed at improving the fiscal health of the United States. He calls climbing health care costs an "emergency" that will consume 22 percent of GDP by 2015, diminishing our global business competitiveness and undermining our economy.[8] According to the CAHR, even by 2008 the average Fortune 500 firm had health care expenses outpacing its net income. In a *Wall Street Journal* article he authored, Burd argues that "market-based" health care solutions (as opposed to government subsidized plans) can reduce the U.S. health care bill by as much as 40 percent.[9] As an example, he points to Safeway's own health care plan (in place since 2005), which has used incentives for healthy behavior to keep the company's per capita health care costs flat for four years, a period in which most other corporations' health care costs have increased 38 percent. The company is even asking for legislation that would allow them to increase their incentives for healthy behavior. For example, Safeway plan members are rewarded $312 annually for avoiding tobacco, but it costs the company an additional $1,400 to insure a tobacco user; they'd like to increase rewards for healthier employees, lowering Safeway's overall health care bill and, in turn, the nation's.

The primary motivator behind Burd's support for universal coverage is not altruism; it's a lower health care bill for Safeway. In 2005, Safeway was spending about $1 billion on health care, more than twice its earnings. Reminiscing about how reluctant corporations were to provide universal coverage when they were the ones expected to provide it, Senator Wyden said, "Now the refrain is, 'We can't afford not to do it.'"[10] For more evidence that big business is supporting coverage for all, look no further than the largest retailer on earth: in the summer of 2009, Walmart CEO Mike Duke threw his support behind the Obama administration and joined with the leaders of the Service Employees International Union and a liberal think tank to call for an *employer mandate* in the proposed health care reform legislation, whereby employers would either have to provide coverage for employees or contribute to a public fund covering the uninsured.[11] CAHR's plan, in contrast, says little about what employers would be required to do under the new system. Wyden's legislation would mandate that employers "cash out" their benefits by raising the wages of employees, who would take responsibility for obtaining their own coverage.[12] It would also allow companies already providing reasonable coverage—like Safeway—to pay slightly less than others into a public insurance fund. Naturally, Safeway employees have been reluctant to perceive Burd's health care vision as free of self-interest, given his history of fighting union groups on insurance issues and the long waits Safeway employees endure before eligibility for coverage (a year for hourly employees).[13] Given that grocery-industry profits are as low as 1 percent of revenues, Burd has every incentive to cut rising benefit costs, especially as Walmart steals more and more of major grocers' share—in fact, Walmart's entry into California was one of the reasons Burd and his team sought to reduce employee benefits in the first place.[14]

Motives aside, Burd's and other CEOs' advocacy of universal coverage reflects an important new trend: businesses across industries joining forces with the government, unions, and other groups to advance policies with strong social value. "Make sure you have a seat at the table," the CAHR website advises corporations across industries. Many are already seated, and more are running toward such efforts, chairs in hand.

The *Innovation*: Why This Strategy Works

Corporations are rethinking the way they work with the public sector: instead of promoting one-sided agenda legislation or asking for handouts, companies are working with governments to solve social problems in ways that reduce risk and generate business advantages. Rather than waiting to be regulated or futilely lobbying against inevitable policies, companies are getting smarter—partnering with government to make change happen in ways that not only move society forward but also ensure a more favorable position for the business. I call this "reverse lobbying." But it's not just about lobbying in the traditional sense. It's much broader than that, taking the form of deep public-private partnerships and direct public advocacy.

Reverse lobbying works for two reasons: first, because social issues now have the power to directly influence profits; and second, because government is more open now than ever before to directly engaging the private sector in solving social problems. Some have referred to this as "lobbying for good" : the idea that companies can benefit by advocating for charitable causes and social issues within the business's operating environment (for example, by improving schools, reforming welfare, or protecting the wetlands).[15] But reverse lobbying goes well beyond the notion of strategic philanthropy, such as when FedEx offered to airlift medical aid to Haiti after the 2010 earthquake, or when GE sent its forensics experts to help identify victims of the south Asian tsunami in 2004. Although these strategies may offer some indirect benefits or long-term strategic business value, reverse lobbying focuses on social change that *directly impacts the success of the core business*.

The *Backstory*: How We Got Here

It wasn't always this way. A number of factors, including the original lobbying, are driving the need for—and success of—reverse lobbying.

1. A Shift from Direct Lobbying to Advocacy

Traditional lobbying is simply not as powerful as it once was. Nor is it as possible. The Lobbying Disclosure Act (LDA), passed in 1995 and amended twice since then, requires federal lobbyists, corporations, trade associations, and others both to register with Congress and to report their activities publicly, theoretically ending the days when secret meetings and cash-filled briefcases led to suddenly favorable industry-related policies. At the same time, much of what might fall under the broad category of lobbying—including public relations, grassroots campaigns, and the strategies discussed in this chapter—is outside the purview of the LDA and other regulations; it is seen more as advocacy than as lobbying.[16]

Over $4 billion is spent on lobbying-related activities every election cycle in the United States, much of it originating from corporations.[17] But a single business today is unlikely to exert much influence on government policy; rather, companies band together, seeking to influence through intermediaries such as industry trade groups like the National Retail Federation and the Produce Marketing Association. But these groups, too, are better off advocating than lobbying. Part of the reason is the increasing negative attention associated with earmarks and pork-barrel politics. The *2010 Congressional Pig Book* documents 9,129 earmarks worth $16.5 billion and features "Oinker Awards," which highlight the most extraordinarily wasteful projects.[18] A fourteen-figure U.S. national deficit is enough to make just about any self-aggrandizing lobbying effort look bad. What's more, American CEOs—once viewed as the captains of industry—are now often perceived to be more like pirates: between the meltdown of the financial markets and the accountability scandals of firms like Enron and Tyco, the media and the public have a decreasing tolerance for "fat cats," especially executives lobbying for a status quo or a future that gives their companies large advantages with no benefits for society.

2. The Government Is Asking Business to Play a Larger Role in Social Change

The recent financial crisis and bailouts have been blunt reminders of how interlinked business and broader society are, or how important a variable business is in the calculus of social change. Just as major banks like Bank of America and insurance giants like AIG relied on taxpayers to save them from bankruptcy, so the government is looking to big business to help solve social problems in a range of areas. In fact, many argue that governments and business *have* to work together to get past "fundamental barriers to a more sustainable economy."[19]

This trend clearly includes the explosion of public-private partnerships for everything from tollway construction to telecommunication networks to ecotourism. But it also includes more subtle links between business and government. As mentioned earlier in the chapter, Walmart's early support of the Obama administration's mandate to require employer-provided health insurance for workers is just one example. The retail behemoth broke from the U.S. Chamber of Commerce and the National Retail Federation to support the policy, and the move was seen as providing great momentum to the government's push to cover the nation's uninsured.[20] Walmart felt it needed to shape the debate, said Leslie Dach, Walmart's EVP of corporate affairs and government relations.[21] Indeed, supporting the legislation may help prevent the institution of other policies that would place greater insurance-related burdens on Walmart and other companies with lower-paid workers. Even more evidence of how much of a two-way street any form of lobbying has become.

3. Increasing Social Expectations of Business

The government isn't the only one expecting more of businesses these days: the entire public is right there, too. The major corporate scandals and crises of recent decades—Enron, Worldcom, Healthsouth, Tyco, through-the-roof banker bonuses, followed by all the bailouts needed because of the banks' risk-taking in the first place, to name a few—have simultaneously decreased trust in corporations and raised expectations for them today. It's a combination of an overcompensation effect motivating both high expectations of the "good," non-scandal-ridden companies, and an extremely watchful eye on the companies that have been perceived as greed-driven and less trustworthy in recent times (for example, investment banks). It all adds up to the obligation of businesses to fulfill a much more expansive and dimensional version of the social contract—largely through working with the government in a highly visible way for social good.

Businesses are also expecting more of themselves, in part because neglecting social issues can be very costly—and carefully attending to them, very profitable. A 2006 *McKinsey Quarterly* article suggested, "Social and political forces, after all, can alter an industry's strategic landscape fundamentally."[22] The study notes that in lieu of waiting for government to decide their fate, companies should take a more proactive role in policy making, helping to shape public priorities and devise solutions to social problems. This will help companies not only to avoid negative fallout from lobbying, but also to profit from dealing with social issues proactively.

Finally, managers and managers-to-be are being trained on ethical standards and the increasing role of business in society. More MBA programs include courses on sustainability, ethics, social entrepreneurship, and corporate social responsibility now than ever before. One indicator is the number of business schools hosting chapters of Net Impact—a student-run nonprofit committed to using the power of business to create a better world.

These nearly doubled between 2000 and 2005. Today, twenty-nine of *BusinessWeek's* top thirty MBA programs offer Net Impact chapters.[23] Net Impact, social business plan competitions, and modern MBA courses are teaching future managers about new ways to integrate society into business strategy.

The *Formula*: How This Strategy Works

Reverse lobbying is about corporations becoming part of the solution, rather than being the problem. It doesn't require that companies give up their direct interests; it's more about pursuing shared interests with policymakers in ways that accrue both social and business value. The following are the key elements of building a successful reverse lobbying strategy:

1. Ask Not What Your Country Can Do for You ...

The best way to determine how your company can use reverse lobbying is to ask your key stakeholders. These are the people and constituencies who have a bona fide expectation of results from your firm. You'd be surprised how seldom companies actually engage these constituencies, particularly in a selfless mode that centers on their social needs. Here's whom you want to talk to:

- *Senior Leadership.* What are the most important social issues for this business? Where can social change add the most value to our key business objectives? Where can we make the most difference? For Safeway CEO Burd, the answer was all too clear: health care. The company was spending almost double its earnings on employee health care costs, and Burd was frustrated with employees' poor health overall: in 2005 he'd even gathered evidence suggesting that 70 percent of health care costs were directly related to behavior.[24] These insights helped motivate Burd not only to offer more incentives for wellness through Safeway's health plan, but also to band together with over sixty fellow corporations to form the Coalition to Advance Healthcare Reform, a key partner for the government on issues including universal coverage.

- *Key Customers.* Which social issues will best engage customers? Where do customers feel the company can make the biggest impact? You may end up with a lot of different answers—if so, focus on your largest customers. That's what many Walmart suppliers are doing. Sustainability is a critical business issue for Walmart: the company now grades its vendors on their packaging and other indicators of social and environmental compliance. Walmart is the biggest "customer" for a large number of its suppliers; as a result, many are responding by making sustainability a key consideration in their social strategy.

- *Investors/Shareholders.* Which issues are most likely to influence the company's future value? Which issues pose the biggest threats to the business? Those are key questions for investors and major shareholders in a company, but businesses frequently forget to engage these players around social issues. With the increased use of environmental, social, and governance criteria on Wall Street and the rising tide of shareholder activism around social issues, from education to obesity, companies should be sure to factor in the effects of these elements on the business more broadly and the specific effects on investors and shareholders. According to the Social Investment Forum, the average level of shareholder support for resolutions on social and environmental issues rose 57 percent from 2005 to 2007, to a record high.[25]

- *Key government leaders.* What are the most pressing concerns of federal, state, and local officials today? Where are key political allies looking for help from your firm specifically or private sector partners more generally? Where can your leadership truly make a difference? In 2006, McDonald's asked these questions to their contacts in the Chinese government (China is of course a key growth market for the business). While working to establish a chapter of Ronald McDonald House Charities (RMHC) in China, RMHC found that President Hu Jintao had encouraged the society at large to do more to assist disabled children and orphaned children, many of whom were living in "child welfare institutions." This was generally unfamiliar territory for RMHC: the organization has played a major role in increasing access to health care for sick children around the world, but it had no specific program for orphans.[26] So RMHC developed a strategic alliance with McDonald's China, to support the launch of Ronald McDonald Foster Villages in China, turning what used to be staff housing in an orphanage into dorm-style villages housing foster parents.[27] Adoptive parents get free housing, and the government pays a stipend allowing one parent to stay home full-time. There are now six Foster Villages and two child centers across China. The project has garnered national admiration and enabled the business to forge deeper relationships with the Chinese government.

Although stakeholder feedback won't always give you the complete answer, it will help inform the strategy of your reverse lobbying efforts. And sometimes the power of engaging your stakeholders lies in the very act of engagement itself. Just by reaching out and letting people know you genuinely care about their interests, you can establish mutual respect and a more beneficial relationship for business.

2. Establish a *Direct* Nexus to Business Value

Remember, reverse lobbying is a business strategy, so these efforts must be designed to advance business objectives. For Safeway and others in the coalition, health care costs have a direct impact on the corporate bottom line. For McDonald's the business benefit was also clear. By working closely with the Chinese government to solve an important social problem in an innovative way, McDonald's charity was more than just run-of-the-mill corporate philanthropy. According to Warren Liu, author of the book *KFC in China: Secret Recipe for Success*, some of the key success factors for companies doing business in China are: (1) the importance of working effectively with the Chinese government, particularly compared with other developed economies; and (2) brand perception—the Chinese concept of *mianzi* commonly translates as "face" or image and is a crucial aspect of consumers' purchasing decisions.[28] Because of the cultural differences in China, what might be considered "social contract" philanthropy in the United States can have a direct impact on business outcomes like reputation and government relations.

Another reason to articulate a clear business linkage is trust. Reverse lobbying is more authentic than many other tactics because companies can be transparent about their business objectives, which establishes in stakeholders—including consumers—a strong "reason to believe." Will people really believe that a financial services firm is genuinely committed to reducing domestic violence? The fact is, stakeholders are generally wary of companies "doing good" purely for the sake of doing good. Contrary to what most executives believe, stakeholders are actually *more* likely to believe a firm's commitment to social change when there is an explicit business motivation. Everyone knows that Safeway has a business reason for supporting health care reform, and it makes them even more credible as a player in advancing that cause.

3. Find the Best Mechanism to Engage the Issue

As mentioned earlier, reverse lobbying doesn't always involve direct government contact—it's more about using a company's "good offices" and resources to help advance a public agenda. Here are some of the ways in which you can reverse lobby effectively.

- *Public-Private Partnerships (PPPs)*. One way that companies reverse lobby is to partner with federal, state, or local governments to help solve a social problem. I can't overemphasize: to be truly impactful, PPPs—and any other reverse lobbying vehicle—should be designed to advance social change that is *directly linked* to a core business interest. Often you don't have to look far for such opportunities: the government readily publicizes them. When Aneesh Chopra (now the country's chief technology officer) was secretary of technology for Virginia, "with one phone call" he forged a PPP with Cox and Comcast Cable "to carry GED classes for free on their on-demand platform, making those available to thousands upon thousands of Virginians."[29] Or, as Cox and Comcast see these citizens, potential new and more satisfied customers. Other PPPs range from the usual suspects, like tollway and other infrastructure projects, to SC Johnson's venture with USAID to enhance the chrysanthemum production of Rwandan farmers through better organization and technical assistance.[30] Why? Because the flower contains pyrethrum, a critical but hard-to-find ingredient in insecticides like SC Johnson's Raid.

- *Promote a Public Agenda*. Companies can also use their brand image, marketing prowess, and product platforms to promote changes in behavior that are socially beneficial or advocated by the government. This goes well beyond cause marketing,

which is typically designed as a product promotion that shunts
a small charitable contribution to a participating nonprofit. For
example, Unilever partnered with several global and regional
public health organizations to promote the public agenda that
hand washing regularly can help curtail deaths from diarrhea
and infection—but also to get their soap into the hands of
millions of potential customers. Safeway and its partners in
the Coalition to Advance Healthcare Reform are advocating
universal coverage and other measures because they stand to
benefit in terms of lower health care costs and healthier, more
productive employees.

• *R&D*. Companies can pledge a portion of their R&D budgets
to innovate business solutions that directly advance public
policy goals and thus gain government endorsement. In 2008,
GE invested $1.4 billion in clean-technology R&D, and their
total investment in the program is more than $4 billion to
date.[31] Such dedication earned GE status as a US EPA and
Department of Energy Star for over five years running. Now
GE's new *healthymagination* project will put billions into R&D
to launch at least one hundred health care innovations to
improve health outcomes while cutting costs.[32] In announcing
the initiative, GE chairman and CEO Jeffrey Immelt said the
company would also commit $2 billion in financing and
$1 billion in related GE technology and information to
enhance health care outcomes in rural and other underserved
areas.[33] This includes a new MSNBC TV program, lower-cost
X-ray machines, an advisory board including two former
Senate majority leaders, and a partnership with the Mayo
Clinic. These R&D investments advance public priorities (by
lowering health care costs) and advantage the business (GE is
better positioned to win lucrative clean-tech and health care
technology contracts).

- *Super Responsibility.* Another form of reverse lobbying involves companies that go beyond the minimum compliance requirements to contain the negative impacts of their business on society or the environment. One example is the Chicago Climate Exchange, a private cap-and-trade market that allows companies to proactively reduce their carbon emissions. Membership in the exchange is entirely voluntary, and, not surprisingly, some of the most active members are from industries creating the most pollution: automotive, chemicals, and coal mining, among others.

4. Be a First Mover and a First Problem-Solver

Initiative counts. In fact, experts in this area assert that consumers can tell the difference between companies that take a more proactive stance toward social responsibility—including reverse lobbying—and those that use responsibility efforts defensively or merely to keep up with peers.[34] So it's a plus that consumers were surprised to see Safeway do a 180-degree turn on their stance regarding federally mandated health care. And being proactive also means trying to solve the problem when others are just making noise about it—even if it's advocacy noise. Safeway CEO Burd not only helped Senator Ron Wyden craft the universal health care legislation, but also launched the Coalition to Advance Healthcare Reform, rounding up over sixty major companies to join it to date, giving the group major clout.

5. Use a Wraparound Strategy to Scale

Companies can scale their reverse lobbying efforts by leveraging other tools and resources including grantmaking, traditional social responsibility efforts, and coalitions. Remember, you don't want to be the only one pushing for reform or any other issue (though you may want to be first). That's why the Chicago Climate Exchange was started explicitly to scale the antipollution effort, and why

Safeway started a coalition rather than taking on the universal health care issue alone.

The *Pitfalls*: What to Watch Out For

There are a number of ways that reverse lobbying can backfire. Above all, the strategy must be genuine and integral to the success of the core business. Here are some of the more common missteps that companies should avoid:

1. Don't Fake It

For this strategy to be effective, your business must have a genuine self-interest in the issue. This bolsters your trustworthiness and enables you to sustain your commitment. As I pointed out in Chapter Five, Enter New Markets Through Backdoor Channels, Exxon and other oil companies fell into a "bottomless pit" of philanthropy by supporting charitable causes in Angola and other African countries that had no direct connection to their business. Not only was there no exit strategy, but there was no upside either. Instead, companies should identify a discrete issue that makes sense for them to solve and has the support of local authorities.

2. Be Careful If You Are Coming from a Place of Low Credibility

Some companies that have been highly criticized by the government or the media may have a more difficult time with this strategy. Instead, you can reverse lobby by being super responsible and addressing these concerns in a highly visible and proactive manner. That's what Nike did in the wake of its infamous child-labor issues, voluntarily implementing a strict code of social responsibility throughout its supply chain that improved working conditions for some seven hundred factories in fifty-two countries.[35] Walmart did the same by launching their sustainability initiative (climate change is a big priority for the federal government) at a time of low credibility.

3. Don't Mistake This for Issues Management

The instinct at some companies may be to consider this an "issues management" or government affairs strategy. That's not what this is about. There are legitimate needs for business to defend against threatening social or regulatory issues, and although reverse lobbying can certainly be deployed as a regulatory strategy, it is designed to be more proactive than defensive.

Through public-private partnerships, support of key legislation, and efforts to promote high-profile policy agendas, businesses like Safeway, Walmart, and GE are creating social benefits and gaining business advantage. As social expectations of corporations continue to grow, companies must continually innovate to find the nexus of public policy goals and the bottom line.

Part III

THE ROADMAP TO SOCIAL INNOVATION

Social innovation is more than just a good idea; it's a way of doing business. To be successful, you'll need to create an enabling environment—a *license to innovate*. This is harder than you may think. Many corporate cultures marginalize the role of social strategy, often relegating it to a support function under human resources or administration. Worse, some senior executives stand resolute in their belief that this work shouldn't be about making money, it's about "doing the right thing." In this part of the book, you'll learn how to overcome these challenges and socialize the concept of social innovation inside your business. You'll also learn the formula for *how* to innovate, whether you adopt one of the five strategies in this book or choose to create your own. We'll get into the nitty-gritty of how to integrate your strategy with the rest of the business, and we'll share key insights from one of the key insiders at McDonald's. Finally, we'll tackle the thorny issue of measuring performance. Too many books simply recite the challenges. Not this one. Here you'll get the tips on how to actually do it.

It's clear that social innovation will have profound implications for the way you run your business. It will also have profound implications for those around you: in particular, socially responsible investors, government, and nonprofits. As companies take on a much bigger role in solving social problems (and tie these efforts to profits), investors will need to fundamentally rethink the way to evaluate social responsibility; nonprofits will need to fundamentally rethink how to raise funds from corporations; and governments will need to fundamentally rethink how to partner with corporations. The final chapter will analyze these implications and offer practical guidance for how each can succeed in this new era.

Chapter 9

CREATING A CULTURE OF SOCIAL INNOVATION

One of my favorite stories is about an executive at a major commercial bank who'd just accepted an appointment as executive vice president of corporate social responsibility. A twenty-year veteran, she had previously headed several different business units, including one of the bank's largest. Soon after she accepted the position—which reported directly to the CEO—she ran into one of the other group presidents in the hallway.

"Why in the world did you take *that* job?" he asked her. "It's a total CLM!"

CLM? "Career limiting move." That's often the attitude you'll find inside major corporations with respect to corporate social anything. The perception is that there's no profit and no business contribution; it's basically a glorified support function. But if you want to make your company a social innovator, you have to change this perception.

It won't be easy. You're likely to confront a number of challenges in moving your company toward social innovation—many to do with logistics, funding, and resources. The single biggest challenge you'll face, however, will be more subtle and intangible: culture. Culture is the backbone of a socially innovative firm, the thing that gives you permission to do this work. And many firms don't have a culture that sees social strategy as a business strategy. In many firms, leadership views corporate responsibility and philanthropy as "just the right thing to do." So in their minds, anything that sounds even vaguely responsibility-related is a support function, not a strategic business unit; it's a cost center that ends up somewhere on the balance sheet under the heading of "goodwill." There's usually a dead giveaway to these types of cultures: when the CSR or community relations function reports into HR or legal.

"No," some will say, "our company is different—our CEO really 'gets it.'" But what exactly does the CEO get? She's values-driven. She's really passionate about doing well by doing good. She serves on the boards of several national nonprofits. She really appreciates the strategic importance of this work. And therein lies the real kicker: she *appreciates* this work, but does she really *value* it? Odds are, most CEOs and boards appreciate the good work that the company does. But because it's just "good work" and not contributing directly to the benefit of the business, they can't really value it.

The business case, although enticing, is more of a retrofit: let's do this good work—give grants, offer employees time off for volunteering, disclose our carbon footprint—and then find a post-hoc business justification to support it. Volunteering helps with employee retention and grant making; other social-responsibility efforts improve our reputation; donating equipment to developing countries could lead to new business—yes, in a broad sense these all might be true. But there are probably other strategies that would yield much more direct, tangible, and measurable business value. And because of this relatively weaker business case, your company will continue to view social responsibility as a "nice to have" support function and will devote to it the minimum resources that it can justify.

I recall working with one community affairs director who was having a tough time convincing her CEO of her team's value. At the time, her group had a budget of $18 million. At the end of 2007, she put in for a 10-percent budget increase. The CEO approved a final budget … for $9 million! Indignant and exasperated, the director called the CEO and demanded an explanation. "Your work has no impact on the business anyway," he said tersely, "so why spend the extra money?" She argued that the company had received many awards and positive press mentions, and employees loved their volunteer work—it made a real difference to the business. He responded with two words: "Prove it." She was dead in the water.

Recently, someone asked me how many companies I thought were doing social innovation. So I went back and analyzed the data from many of the clients I've worked with and hundreds of companies I've taught. Turns out that approximately 60 percent of companies fall into what I call "CSR 1.0" (traditional philanthropy and compliance); 35 percent fall into what I call "CSR 2.0" (some level of strategic philanthropy or sustainability); and only about 5 percent or less are doing social innovation, or what I refer to as "CSR 3.0." Even so, many in CSR 3.0 are there by accident—for example, Walmart's $4 generic prescription program turned out to be a major social innovation, but it wasn't designed to be one. Walmart's work on sustainability, on the other hand, is purely social innovation.

Minding the Gaps

So how can you change your company culture so that it embraces social innovation? There are three critical gaps to close in changing the culture: language, expectations, and skills. Let's take a closer look at each.

The Language Gap

Many managers working on social responsibility, sustainability, or philanthropy tend to speak a different language from the rest of the business. Here's a great illustration of that point. While advising a Fortune 1000 company, I interviewed both the director of corporate citizenship and the CEO. I asked them the same two questions: what does the business value most from its citizenship work, and how would you measure its impact on the business? Here's what the director of corporate citizenship told me:

> *Valued impact:* We value authentic social change, institutional or public policy change. We are long-term thinking, forward looking, trying to intersect future forces. We want to be leaders in the field. Our role is to learn the triggers of change, to seed new ideas, to earn a reputation for being progressive, to expand our community footprint, our reach. We focus on finding the right partners.
>
> *Measures of success:* It's about scalability. The reach of our work (number of people served). Our visibility and reputation among nonprofits and grantees.

Now, here's a paraphrase of how the CEO answered:

> *Valued impact:* I'm looking for the best use of our dollars. This work needs to add value to our brand perception. It must be linked to the strategic business plan. There needs to be a clear business case. If done right, it should impact the top line of the business. We need to show the link between business growth and giving. We are focused on sustained commercial success, and creating a culture that draws the best talent. The focus needs to be on our CSR reputation, the impact on consumer willingness to buy, and how we can leverage our retail stores.
>
> *Measures of success:* I want quantitative measures of our CSR reputation among consumers and employees. How much money we have saved for the company. The contribution we've made to employee retention and productivity.

Hard to believe that both of these executives were from the same company! I also remember another conversation I had with the director of corporate citizenship:

"They just don't get it," she said of the company's business leadership. "They understand environment because it saves us money, but they just don't get social change."

I remember thinking, *It's not the business's job to "get it"—it was her job to "get" the business and promote strategies that truly contributed to it!* Due to disconnects like these, the director of corporate citizenship was let go at the end of the year.

As the example suggests, inside companies we continue to speak two different languages—one for business and one for responsibility. Here's another great example of the chasm between them. At a company I advised, which was in the midst of a turnaround, the CSR director made a presentation to the senior leadership team. He bragged that the firm had reached one hundred thousand employee volunteer hours. Rather than patting him on the back or even smiling, the CEO noted, "That just sounds like a hundred thousand hours that people aren't working!" So, though we often speak different languages, business has only one: the language of business! To be effective, social innovators must learn how to translate their work into the language of business.

How can you translate your work into the language of the business? It's simple: put it into terms that the business values. In the preceding example, I advised the CSR director to translate the number of employee volunteer hours (a meaningless metric to the business) into something that the business *did* value: the percentage of employees who are "highly engaged," as evidenced by volunteering, serving on a community involvement team, and expressing buy-in to the core values of the business. Those employees, research shows, work harder, exert discretionary effort, and are likely to stick around longer. We were able to show that 20 percent of the employees were highly engaged. This time the CEO was genuinely excited: "Great!" he said. "Let's get that number to 50 percent next year!" Language makes a big difference.

The Expectations Gap

Here's an astonishing statistic: according to a survey conducted in 2009, 56 percent of investment professionals and CFOs, when asked whether CSR improves shareholder value, answered yes. Now here's the shocker: 53 percent of CSR *professionals* answered a shoulder-shrugging "I don't know."[1] If the social capital market—and our employers—expect us to deliver shareholder value through social strategy, but we don't even know whether we are doing so, the odds are good that we aren't!

There are two expectations gaps: one in which the company doesn't expect any business value from this work, and one in which the company expects much greater value than this work is currently delivering. To succeed in either scenario, social innovators will need to bridge that gap and establish clear expectations for performance and a common understanding of success for this work.

Remember, an utter lack of expectations—or indifference to responsibility or social innovation efforts—isn't such a good thing either. After one of my workshops, a community affairs director said, "Well, why should I worry about tracking our performance metrics? My CEO has never even asked me for any!" My response: "If he's not asking, you should worry!" If the CEO doesn't care to know how you're performing, that's an indicator that he probably doesn't value your work. It's just a write-off for the business. You're being appreciated, not *valued*. And in an economic slump, that's not a good place to be.

Whether or not your leadership has clear expectations for your work, it's likely that your company does not view social change as a *business strategy*. To be successful, you need to change this. To borrow a term from CSR, you don't need a license to operate, you need a license to *innovate!* I outline the steps you'll need to take a bit later.

The Skills Gap

The final gap has to do the core competencies needed to succeed with social innovation. These may be very different from the skills required to serve effectively in social contract functions—skills like philanthropy, compliance reporting, and community involvement (such as volunteering). Many of the people doing social contract work have nonprofit experience, grant-making experience, or skills in policy, program design, or evaluation. Others may have a more generalized skill set, such as public relations, communications, human relations, legal, or even an auditing background, if their role is more technical (for example, supply chain monitoring or compliance). And then there are the people that end up in this line of work purely by happenstance. These backgrounds satisfy the current needs of a social contract function, but they don't necessarily serve the needs of a social innovation function. Successful social innovation requires three core competencies:

- *A head for business:* You've got to understand the mechanics of business, what the incentives are, how performance is measured, how decisions get made, the way markets work, and key trends in management.

- *Strategic thinking:* You've got to be able to analyze complex problems, drill down to the root of a problem, understand how to integrate disparate concepts, think creatively, formulate a strategy, and develop a business case.

- *Leadership skills:* You've got to be able to articulate a vision, inspire people to follow that vision, make compelling arguments to those in power, mobilize resources, communicate with passion, and manage people effectively.

It's not necessarily the case that every person involved in social innovation needs to have *all* of these skills at once, but these skills must be well-represented on the social innovation team. It certainly helps if you have a background in social change or some exposure to it. But as I frequently tell students applying for jobs in the CSR field: there is no such thing as being really good at "nonprofits"—nonprofit is a category, not a skill. That said, experience with the social sector is invaluable and critical to success in social innovation. You've got to know which levers to pull, how to make change happen, who the players are, and how to effectively forge high-value partnerships and alliances.

Many of the skills just listed resemble the skills of a business unit leader. That's not a coincidence: success with social innovation requires the same skills as success with any kind of business innovation because it is a form of business innovation. And the unit-level skills are important because to drive success, social innovators must transform CSR, citizenship, community affairs, sustainability, and corporate philanthropy functions into *strategic business units*. These business units must operate on the same basis as any other, with a budget that ties directly to the bottom line of the firm, a clear set of performance measures, goals that line up directly with key business priorities, and a strategy that the business can understand.

How to Create a Culture of Social Innovation

So given where you are at today, how you can overcome these gaps and change the culture of your organization to create a "license to innovate"?

1. Master the Business

Job one is to understand the fundamentals of your business. Your credibility in convincing the business to mobilize its resources in pursuit of any strategy relies on your understanding of the underlying drivers of the core business. Consider the case of a major American clothing retailer, whose community relations team was considered a leader in social responsibility. During a strategy session it became clear that this world-class team was quite detached from the rest of the business. The staff had no connection with company's marketing and operations units, and couldn't even name the business's largest customers or best selling SKU's (stock-keeping units, or items for sale). This lack of basic knowledge about the core business isolated the department's work in a silo and limited their ability to leverage the business.

Bottom line: if you want to influence the business, you have to know what makes it tick. Where are the biggest sources of revenue? Who are the top twenty customers? Who is your target demographic? Where are the emerging markets, the biggest growth opportunities? What are the CEO's top three business priorities? What is the company's reputation among employees, consumers, business partners? What is the language of the business? What are the key performance metrics?

2. Engage Key Stakeholders

Whenever I work with clients, I'm always surprised at how few of them have ever really engaged the business leadership in a direct conversation about the business leaders' expectations for social change–related work. The first step to changing the culture is to put it out there that you want to be relevant and aligned with the business. Ask which business outcomes they think you can best contribute to. Come with your own ideas as well.

The act of engaging people also has another benefit: it plants the seed and creates a level of awareness about your intentions to align more closely with the business. Use these discussions to explain the concept of social innovation. Determine who views your role or function as strategic and who sees it as a traditional, "do good" support function. These conversations will also help you determine who is going to be your champion inside the business. During a stakeholder interview at one large retailer I advised, the senior vice president of advertising got so excited about social innovation that he declared, "This is my biggest priority for 2010." He was a good champion to have—the company's advertising budget for 2010 was over half a billion dollars!

Something to keep in mind: sometimes the word "stakeholder" is interpreted too broadly. By stakeholders, I mean those who have a *bona fide expectation of results* from your company. These include senior management, key business partners, key customers, Wall Street analysts, investors, and employees. Here are the questions you will want to ask them:

- Which social issues are most relevant to our company's growth?

- Where do you think we can make the biggest difference?

- What business outcomes do you think are most relevant to our work?

- How would you measure our success?

- What data can we show you to demonstrate that success?

3. Reengage with Your Team

Not only do you have to move the business to a different way of thinking, but you also need to get your own team on board. Share the vision of social innovation; get them excited about playing a larger (and more strategic) role in the business. Get their creativity flowing. Get their buy-in. Determine your team strengths: do you have the skills necessary to succeed? Also, identify your team's assets: key partners, expertise on social issues, business backgrounds, standing in the community, access to external resources, political relationships, media contacts, and so on. Knowing these will help you inform the strategy and redeploy your assets more strategically. One client, a commercial lender, used an "asset mapping" strategy and soon realized that they had direct relationships with executives at ten of the top twenty companies on the bank's high-value target list!

When you engage your team, you will invariably confront skepticism, fear, and sometimes dissension (during one such conversation, I heard a program manager announce, "I'm not here to help the company make more money; I'm here to save the world!"). You will also need to both allay fears and align your team with a common set of goals. And in some cases you may need to redirect folks to a different career path.

4. Put a Stake—or Several—in the Ground

If you want the business to view your work more like that of a business unit, you need to start acting like a business unit. Based on your feedback and assets, articulate clear goals and metrics that are aren't just "aligned" with the business but *directly* drive the business. Make them known to everyone. This will go a long way toward resetting people's expectations. In the earlier example of the major clothing retailer, the community relations department had never participated in the company-wide strategic business planning (SBP) process. As part of their transformation into a business unit, the department decided to participate in that process; it completed the same SBP template used by every other business unit. The community relations SBP detailed the department's key strategies and how those strategies aligned with top corporate priorities, and enumerated their key initiatives, business drivers, and performance metrics. This little step went a long way toward changing the way the rest of the business viewed the department's work. Support functions don't do business plans; business units do. So make sure you change the way you communicate, to speak the language of the business. Start sending your performance metrics to key leadership, even if they don't ask for them. If you make the effort to "get" the business, most likely it will begin to better "get" you.

5. Pilot-Test an Innovation

The most powerful way to create a culture of social innovation is to demonstrate that it can produce real results. No one could argue with the impact of Walmart's sustainability initiative: when the company cut its packaging by 5 percent, that equated to taking

210,000 diesel-powered trucks off the road; when it made its fleet 38 percent more efficient in 2008, that cut the expense of ninety million miles of transportation across the United States.[2] Nor could anyone argue with the $100 million in revenues generated through Unilever's Shakti initiative, the $500 million in revenues from Coca-Cola's MDC, or the 99 percent of OfficeMax employees who said taking part in A Day Made Better made them proud to work for the company.

To get results like these, you'll need to take some risks. In 2009, the Walgreens drugstore company launched a small pilot to begin stocking fresh fruits, vegetables, and other healthy options in select "food desert" locations in Chicago, an initiative that grew out of a request from the municipality after supermarkets left several urban areas with few food options.[3] Seeing the opportunity to solve a social problem while driving new revenues, Walgreens shrank the photo department to make space for shelves and freezers to accommodate the produce and other products like pasta. Through pilots in ten stores, the company gathered data that showed some marked improvement in sales of those items, and the initiative has already been expanded to other regions.

Bottom line: your strategy doesn't need to be perfected to begin influencing the culture and creating your license to innovate. Get some traction, collect relevant data, and put others on notice that you're in the business of social innovation.

Chapter 10

THE FORMULA FOR SOCIAL
INNOVATION

Social innovation doesn't depend on a brilliant epiphany or investing billions of dollars in bold, breakthrough ideas. It's a mind-set, an approach, and a way of doing business that anyone can adopt. To do social innovation right, you need more than just the five strategies outlined in this book—you need an enabling environment (the subject of Chapter Nine), a roadmap for determining the right strategy, guidelines on how to integrate your work with the rest of the business, and a language in which to communicate your value (measurement). This chapter walks you through those steps and teaches you how to design your own social innovation strategies and bring them to life within your organization.

Selecting the Right Social Innovation Strategy

So how do you get started? Which strategy makes the most sense for your company? What if you have a very limited budget for social impact work? What if you are a B2B company and don't have consumers? What if your company is in trouble financially? What if you're in a "socially irresponsible" industry or starting from a place of low credibility? While every company faces different constraints and opportunities, I think it's best to start with the basics when developing social innovation strategies, particularly if this is new territory for you—as it is for most businesses. Luckily, there is a universal set of basic steps to designing the most effective social innovation strategy. And here it is.

Step One: Determine the Key Business Outcomes

Social innovation always starts with a clear business driver. For WellPoint, the business driver was the need to find a fresh customer base. For Tesco, it was entering the U.S. market. For OfficeMax, it was growing share and loyalty within a profitable, competed-for segment. For Travelers, it was about acquiring the talent to stay relevant to changing demographics. For Safeway, it was cost reduction. Remember that social innovation differs from other strategies that "do the right thing" first and then look for a business justification. With social innovation, you always start with the business premise first. There are no limits to the types of business outcomes that social innovation can drive, but the most common ones are consistent with the five strategies I've outlined in this book:

- Create revenues through submarket products and services.

- Enter new markets through backdoor channels.

- Build emotional bonds with customers.

- Develop new pipelines for talent.

- Influence policy through reverse lobbying.

To determine your company's key business outcomes, engage your stakeholders (see Chapter Nine for tips); often they will give you the answer directly. In other cases, you may need to zero in on the subset of key business priorities that make the most sense for social strategy. For example, assume that one of your company's business priorities was expanding your customer "share of wallet" (that is, the amount of their discretionary income that they spend on your products) through expanded offerings. Social innovation may be better positioned to contribute to this outcome by innovating new products or services. Or you may be better positioned to focus on deepening customer loyalty (and thereby expanding share of wallet) through emotive customer bonding. Either way, you will get to the same business outcome.

Step Two: Analyze the Social Issues That Drive Your Business

The next step is to find the nexus of your business outcomes and social change. This almost always requires research—even for companies that may feel like the answer is obvious. For example, one large retailer was convinced that the most important issue to their customers was sustainability and the environment. It was all over the media, the retailer was continually beset with criticism from NGOs and activists, and their environmental footprint was huge. Still, when we researched the question with consumers, they felt no "emotional bond" to the issue and didn't feel like that was the social problem the company was best suited to solve. At the same time, not all research involves consumer surveys. Sometimes this research can be done within the business, asking key business unit heads (e.g., sales, operations, human resources, marketing) which social issues will contribute most directly to their business strategy. For Safeway, the issue presented itself: Safeway was spending more on health care costs than it made in profits! In other cases, the research can be conducted through stakeholder engagement in target markets, with key business partners, or with investors.

Identifying the big-picture social issue is just the first part of this step. Next you must analyze the issue more carefully to tease out the specific outcome that you can own. For OfficeMax, the company's position wasn't just generally, abstractly pro-education; it made a choice to use the business to support teachers in underfunded classrooms with much-needed supplies, so that teachers were not spending their own paychecks when school budgets fell short. The issue was both ownable and important to their prototypical customer "Eve"—for whom they tried to tailor offerings—making it a key business priority. Same with Tesco. The company could have supported the charitable issue of hunger with donations of money and employees' time, but instead they forged a nexus between a social outcome (solving food deserts) and their business interests (entering the U.S. market).

Step Three: Identify the Core Business Assets You Can Leverage

Every business has multiple assets—people, brand, customers, products, relationships, and so on. But your company has only a few *core* assets. The core business is the fulcrum in social innovation. It's what allows social innovation to have exponential impact over those of philanthropy or other noncore assets. And it's what enables the social innovation strategy to benefit the business directly. For Coca-Cola, their distribution channel is a core business asset, which enabled the manual distribution center model to become a social innovation. For Unilever, their core business asset is their sales force, which enabled the formation of high-performing Shakti representatives in Indian villages. For Walmart, it was their purchasing power, which enabled the $4 generic prescription program. For Tesco, it was the business itself, providing fresh food, which enabled them to transform food deserts into a social innovation.

Once you've identified the business outcome and the social outcome, you can work with your team to identify the core business assets that can be brought to bear on solving the problem. This is also a great opportunity for you to put to use the skills you learned in Chapter Nine, Creating a Culture of Social Innovation: mastering the business, engaging stakeholders, and reengaging with your team.

Step Four: Innovate

The final step may be the toughest, but it's where the magic happens. Social innovation requires an intuitive leap—a discovery of hidden value and untapped potential that isn't always apparent to the naked eye. In each of the cases I've outlined in this book, someone saw business value in social change where others did not. That's the "social arbitrage" I mentioned earlier. Cisco saw value in jobless inner-city kids who could help support their business growth throughout the world by becoming trained technicians. Tesco and Walgreens both found value in food deserts. Unilever found value in eliminating disease through hand washing. Walmart found value in making generic prescription drugs cheaper and more accessible to the uninsured (and everyone else). Pampers found value in eliminating tetanus among babies and pregnant moms in developing countries. Innovation is about combining your creativity, ingenuity, and business pragmatism to create value by lowering costs, developing new products, changing behavior, forging new relationships, and influencing policy.

This book identifies the five most common social innovation strategies, and provides you with the insights, tips, and case examples that you can use to inform your strategy. But you need not be limited to these strategies. Indeed, innovation should always be a creative endeavor—one that results in a novel idea, solution, or strategy. So you should feel free to create your own social innovation strategies. Here are some tips or thought-starters you can use, pulled from the strategy chapters:

- *Find the economic potential.* For a desired social change, ask yourself, "Who would pay for this?" WellPoint realized that the young invincibles *would* pay for health care insurance if the company designed a product that demonstrated sufficient value. Safeway and Walmart realized that they could pay themselves to change certain social and environmental behaviors. Walgreens discovered that people in food deserts will pay for fresh fruit and vegetables if someone makes it convenient to do so.

- *Find a sugar daddy.* Sometimes you can come up with a great idea but the start-up costs may seem prohibitive (not everyone has GE's or Tesco's pocketbook). So another way to arbitrage value is to find others who are willing to help cover the costs of the social change you're aiming for. Safeway created a coalition of thirty-six major companies to share in its advocacy efforts. Pampers enlisted the help of moms. Small grocers now have the potential to tap into $400 million in subsidies through the U.S. government's Healthy Food Financing Initiative. OfficeMax was able to tap the goodwill of their suppliers to cover some of the costs related to their A Day Made Better initiative. There are dozens of new state and federal initiatives encouraging companies to invest in new "green" and medical technologies. If you can create a shared value proposition, odds are someone will be willing to help pay the freight.

- *Microfy.* As we mentioned in Chapter One, you can use this strategy to modify existing products or services and simplify them for new markets. The key to this innovation lies in the 20/80 rule: identifying the 20 percent of functionality that meets 80 percent of the need. The 20/80 rule worked for Tonik: WellPoint pared down the insurance by removing maternity coverage, a high-cost item of little value to their young target segment. Walmart was able to microfy someone else's product—using their pricing power to bring down the cost of generic prescription drugs, thereby providing well over 80 percent of the functionality at approximately 20 percent of the cost.

• *Redeploy your core competencies.* Sometimes, transferring what you already know to new markets can create value too. That's what GE is doing with its *healthymagination* initiative, aiming its hefty R&D budget at reducing health care costs. And that's what Salesforce.com is doing for nonprofits by creating customized solutions for them.

• *Use "trickle-up" innovation.* You can try new products and services in alternative markets and then "upstream" successful ideas to more established markets or to larger scales. In Chapter Four, Create Revenues Through Submarket Products and Services, I discussed how GE tested a smaller-scale electrocardiograph machine in China and India, then modified it for use in more developed markets like the United States, saving a lot of time and money. It is likely that, based on the success of smaller-format stores in U.S. food deserts, Tesco could expand its Fresh & Easy Neighborhood Market concept to developing markets, or slowly increase the size of the stores to compete even more directly with supermarkets, or both.

• *Create distribution and jobs.* Job creation is an easy way to innovate. Coca-Cola's manual distribution centers in Africa employ many Africans as managers and delivery people, giving them job opportunities that didn't exist several years ago. Hindustan Unilever's Shakti representatives—who generate close to $100 million annually for the company—are rural women the company recruited based on their interest in microcredit and other empowerment opportunities.

Other times, such opportunities are a natural result of a strategy aimed at a different outcome, as when Tesco created jobs for cashiers and others at new stores in U.S. food deserts. The point is to think broadly, innovatively, and with an eye toward creating social value to solve distribution and talent problems for your business.

- *Increase access to social products, services, or messages.* Another way to innovate is to leverage your business platform to increase access to vital products and services. Coca-Cola is considering using its distribution channels in developing markets to carry "social" products (such as rehydration salts)—both on its own and through partnerships with nonprofits like ColaLife. Lifebuoy soap was able to dovetail its business goals with public health needs by promoting hand washing.

Integrating with the Business

Once you've determined your social innovation strategy, you will need to focus on integrating your efforts with the rest of the business in order to bring it to scale. Fifty percent of integration will be accomplished through building a culture of innovation, as discussed in Chapter Nine. The other half requires getting the broader business invested in making your social innovation a success.

In 2006, McDonald's launched an Activation Team to integrate the Ronald McDonald House Charities strategy with the rest of the business. The team was led by a savvy business insider who reported directly to the president of McDonald's USA. The insider's name was Chuck Scott—and with more than thirty-five years at McDonald's, Chuck knew how to make things happen, leading the Activation Team with surgical precision, confidence, and deft diplomacy. I sat down with Chuck to ask him how he did it. Here are his key insights:

1. *Understand the way of the business.* It's important to talk about your work in terms that the business can understand. Internally, McDonald's focused its operations around the "five P's": people, products, place, price, promotion. Chuck lined up the RMHC initiatives with the five P's, so that it was clear where social strategies could plug in.

2. *Integrate for sustainability.* Make sure you have a wide range of businesspeople involved on the team so that the work becomes self-perpetuating. Chuck pulled in people from all parts of the business and also made sure that the RMHC team didn't rely on just one representative.

3. *Add value.* Simply put, your social innovation strategy can't be a distraction to the business. To be taken seriously, it must help advance key business priorities. So Chuck's team had to find ways of demonstrating direct and immediate business benefits by finding quick wins and reporting frequent results.

4. *Focus on small wins.* While many social innovations may carry a big vision, it's critical to start with small, achievable steps and quick wins to show quick traction. One way that McDonald's did this was by redesigning crew uniforms to include small RMHC patches and hang tags—a step that offered immediate benefits for employee morale.

5. *Make it easy.* The business doesn't have time to break down big concepts and figure out how to absorb them, so make ideas easily digestible. Chuck explains: "If it has to go through a lot of people and different levels, the chance of integration is slim." For example, McDonald's created a library of stock photos about RMHC that owner-operators of McDonald's restaurants could easily grab and post on store bulletin

boards and in the lobby so customers could see how the local owner-operator supported the charity.

6. *Use consistent messaging.* You have to keep the profile high, the communications steady, and the messages simple. It's called "socializing" the concept within the business. McDonald's made sure to mention the team's work in every edition of their manager's newsletter and ensured that top management included comments related to the work in their internal and external speeches.

7. *Get buy-in from the "users."* It's essential to engage the people in the business who will be most affected by your initiative. Solicit their input, ask their advice on how to overcome hurdles they raise, and find ways to make their jobs easier. At McDonald's, Chuck made sure to include crew members in the discussions about uniform designs to integrate RMHC's identity.

8. *Get the right people on the team.* Too often people will volunteer for teams but fail to follow through. It's important to involve those who have clout in their functional areas but not so much clout that they won't have time to show up. Drop those on the team who can't fully participate early. On day one, Chuck discussed when the team would finish its work and what the end products would look like, making sure everyone was committed to these targets and clearly understood the final goal.

9. *Secure visible and constant support from leadership.* Integration efforts often involve extra time, sacrifices, budget changes, and sometimes even job reassignments. Having solid support from senior leadership helps to ease these transitions and give the team confidence that the work is worth the price. In addition to management, McDonald's leadership owner-operators enlisted the support of high-profile peers to give others confidence.

10. *Communicate results*. Early traction is critical. Communicating early wins and positive results helps to build support and silence the naysayers. McDonald's conducted "GAP" studies to show increases in customer awareness and revisit-intent—metrics that matter deeply to owner-operators.

These integration lessons work for both large corporations and smaller companies, and they apply to major, ambitious efforts and more circumscribed ones. It's also important to note that integration isn't just a functional effort; it's a culture-building experience too. Every interaction with the business is an opportunity to set expectations about your work and move from appreciation to value.

Measuring Performance

Measurement has gained new significance in the social capital market. Before, in the social contract world, measurement for corporate social strategy was about accountability (or "CYA" as some companies called it—covering your "behind"). To demonstrate accountability, many of the companies I know have been tracking compliance with various social responsibility standards, such as those established by the Dow Jones Sustainability Index, the FTSE 4 Good index, or the Global Reporting Initiative. Companies have also tried to demonstrate accountability by engaging universities to conduct large-scale program evaluations of their philanthropic initiatives. These research projects often take several years to complete, costing hundreds of thousands of dollars. And most end up on a shelf somewhere in a fancy binder. Unread. Yet for many companies, it was a good CYA mechanism—at least they could prove that grant dollars weren't wasted! In today's social capital market, accountability-style measurement is falling out of favor; stakeholders are more concerned with positive social change (and its related business value) than efforts to do good—or to do less bad.

In the past, measuring business value was challenging for corporate social practitioners because most strategies they were assessing
hadn't been designed to produce that kind of value in the first
place. I often found my clients trying to go through all kinds of
statistical gymnastics to show that a grant to the Boys and Girls
Clubs was going to create more sales, or improve its reputation
with customers, or retain X percent of employees. It won't. It's just
a good thing to do. And there's nothing wrong with that. When we
liberate ourselves from the impossible task of stretching our social
contract strategies to become business strategies, we also liberate
ourselves from the impossible task of measurement.

What's different about measurement in the social capital market
is that we now know what "good" is. And that makes the job of
measurement much easier. If good is solving social problems in
a way that creates sustainable business value, then most of the
social and business metrics are going to be the same. WellPoint can
measure the number of formerly uninsured customers that purchase
Tonik and know that the business is growing, and—by virtue of
that growth—serving the needs of an underserved market. Same
with Tesco: the number of new customers it acquires in food deserts
has both business and social significance. Others, like Walmart,
can measure their reduction in carbon emissions and know that
they are both saving money and reducing their impact on the
environment.

The market is already picking up on this new *systemic* approach
to measurement. Goldman Sachs and others are measuring environmental, social, and governance information (ESG) statistics about
companies, under the built-in premise that ESG performance
correlates to business performance. Investors like Generation
Investment Management (the firm run by Al Gore and David
Blood) are measuring sustainability data that factor directly into
long-term business profitability. But this field is still nascent, and
companies can do their part to further it by developing and

communicating simple, clear metrics that demonstrate the real value they are creating for both society and for shareholders.

Here are some tips you can use to develop the right performance measures for your social innovation strategy.

- *Translate strategies into outcomes.* Many practitioners end up measuring the strategies instead of the outcomes. Remember, strategies are the activities you will undertake (for example, develop a product, open a store, launch a coalition). Outcomes are the *resulting changes* in status, behavior, or condition from those activities. There are business outcomes (for example, increasing revenues, saving money, reducing employee turnover) and there are social outcomes (such as reducing the number of uninsured, increasing access to vital services, creating jobs). Stakeholder engagement will help you determine the outcomes that are most valuable for your business. But sometimes you will need to break down larger issues (such as hunger) into component outcomes that you can measure (increasing access to fresh food).

- *Don't sweat proving causation.* Often practitioners will take measurement too seriously, attempting to prove to a statistical certainty that their strategy or intervention is the *only* reason a particular result occurred. Proving causation is not necessary. Social strategy practitioners tend to hold themselves to academic standards of certainty, as opposed to business standards of certainty. I can assure you, no one in public relations can prove, to the exclusion of any other factor, that reputation improved solely because of a celebrity endorsement. But they can show a correlation and an improvement of reputation scores after the endorsement. The key for social strategy is to show a *substantial contribution* to the outcome. It may be hard to prove that WellPoint's Tonik initiative is the only reason why the number of uninsured has decreased in the state of California, but the initiative most certainly made a substantial contribution to that outcome.

- *Use the measures of the business.* You don't need to reinvent the business-metrics wheel. If there are clearly understood performance metrics for your business, measure against those rather than creating new ones. For example, OfficeMax already tracks the number of *MaxPerks* sign-ups as an indicator of customer loyalty, so it made sense for ADMB to use that. Walmart measured improvements in its pharmacy market share, something the company was already tracking, to show that the $4 prescription program made a difference.

- *Create a smart proxy.* Sometimes there is no obvious measure for what you're trying to capture. In those cases, you can create a proxy—a placeholder metric to show your strategy's contribution to a hard-to-measure or distant outcome. For example, Travelers created a pipeline to measure the number of students "on track" for eventual employment at the company. Each stage of the pipeline had different "gating" criteria (for example, a certain grade point average, or a concentration in economics). McDonald's has traditionally measured the total amount donated to in-store RMHC canisters as an indicator of awareness or loyalty. When I visited a store, though, I noticed that many people used the canisters as a repository to dump loose pocket change. I recommended that RMHC proxy customer loyalty instead be measured by the number of dollar bills in the canisters, as that was a better proxy to indicate a specific intent. Some proxies are better than others: in an earlier chapter I talked about using the number of "highly engaged employees" as a proxy for employee engagement with the business instead of tracking the total number of employee volunteer hours. The key is to find the proxy that best captures the true *benefit* of your strategy, rather than measuring the strategy itself.

- *Be credible*. Sometimes people will try to stretch their impact too far and end up compromising their credibility. Particularly in an "old school" culture, credibility is critical, as many in the business may be reluctant to view social strategy as a legitimate contributor to the business.

If there's one thing I've learned from years of measuring social impact, it's that it's not about the measurement; it's about the culture. Social innovation is the same. It's not about waiting to find the perfect strategy; success in social innovation is about adopting the right mind-set. Only then will the tools and teachings of this book be possible.

Chapter 11

IMPLICATIONS OF THE SOCIAL CAPITAL MARKET

In 2010, Pepsi ended its twenty-three-year streak of advertising during the Super Bowl; instead, Pepsi opted to spend more than $20 million on a year-long, consumer-driven cause-marketing campaign called the "Pepsi Refresh Project." The company said that it hoped to achieve "deeper consumer engagement" with the Refresh project.[1] Sound familiar? What Pepsi's move suggests is that the social capital market is here to stay, and it's playing an increasingly mainstream role in the economy. We now see manifestations of the social capital market everywhere—on magazine covers and in newspaper headlines, analyst reports, business school classes, political campaigns, and employee surveys.

But as markets mature, they inherently become more rational. And rational capital markets value performance, not just effort. Now that everyone is doing good, or at least trying to, the market must develop more sophisticated ways to value these efforts. This is already happening. In the last two years alone, the environmental, social, and governance (ESG) investment research industry has attracted the interest of major players: RiskMetrics Group acquired Innovest Strategic Value Advisors and KLD Research & Analytics; Thomson Reuters acquired ASSET4, a Swiss-based ESG investment research provider; and Bloomberg launched an ESG data service for its own subscribers.

Three important themes in the social capital market will have broad-ranging implications for the business of social change *and* the business of business:

- *Smarter allocation of resources.* The rise of the social capital market signals the first time true market discipline will be imposed on social change. Foundations and donors have no effective way to evaluate the value or impact of their investments in nonprofits; it's the same with citizens and government. As the market finds better ways to value social strategies, these methodologies (and expectations) will spill over into government and nonprofit work, demanding greater accountability for results of dollars invested.

- *Solving social problems.* The new emphasis on social solutions (versus efforts) will set a much higher bar for government and nonprofit players, much as it has for corporations. As the private sector emerges as a major force in social change, with the potential to solve the same problems as government and nonprofits, these sectors will have to develop new strategies for partnering with business.

- *Direct link to business value.* The social capital market has proven that there are ways that social change can be *directly linked* to financial performance (that is, social innovation). This will marginalize other strategies that loosely imply a business linkage such as strategic CSR, values-driven investing, and cause marketing. Companies and nonprofit or public sector partners will need to reevaluate the way they work together to achieve higher social impact and more direct business value.

In fact, the penumbras of the social capital market stretch well beyond corporate strategy. Socially responsible investing, the nonprofit sector, and government will each need to substantially rethink the way social value is created and measured. What follows are the implications I foresee in these major areas.

The Social Contract: Exercise the Option to Renew

Throughout this book I have argued that social contract strategies are not relevant in a social capital market. And although it is true that philanthropy and compliance do not drive business growth, this does not mean that the social contract is not relevant. In fact, today these responsibilities are more important than ever. The same trend that is fueling the social capital market—the sheer size of corporations and their ubiquity in our daily lives—is also increasing the importance of corporate responsibility and ethics. The unprecedented influence that corporations wield over society's natural resources, our health, our human rights, our standard of living, and our children *demands* that companies be held to even higher standards of responsibility than ever before. To do so, we will need to develop new, more effective market regulation mechanisms, like cap-and-trade systems, financial incentives, investment criteria, more organized "consumer" lobby groups, and better-trained managers. Self-regulation and squishy CSR standards will go only so far.

Corporate philanthropy and volunteering are important too. Just as business profits by exploiting society's natural resources, it also profits by exploiting society's *human* resources and the infrastructure society has built to maintain those human resources. These include public education, public safety, public health, medical research, social services, the arts, academia, and more. The social contract protects our natural resources, requiring that companies take precautions to minimize their negative footprint on our climate and our ecosystem. But the social contract also protects our *human* resources, requiring that companies give back to the community groups and support the infrastructure that makes it possible for companies to run effectively. Yet corporate taxes do not nearly suffice to recoup these costs (the average state corporate income tax rate in the U.S. is 6.6 percent).[2] Companies must continue to support local nonprofits, cultural institutions, and community-based organizations, particularly those that produce outcomes that government and business cannot.

Socially Responsible Investing: Shift from Ethics to Business Value

The social capital market will likely force a reboot of the entire socially responsible investment (SRI) industry. Currently the vast majority of those trillions of dollars invested in "socially screened" investments are not necessarily producing positive social impact or business value. They were never designed to, because most SRI funds were developed using a social contract mind-set. SRI today is based primarily on *values*, not value. According to Peter Kinder, a founder of research firm KLD Research & Analytics, socially responsible investing is based on the "incorporation of ethical, religious, social and moral values in investment decision making."[3] The majority of funds focus on negative screens that exclude what are seen as socially *irresponsible* corporations, including tobacco companies, defense contractors, those involved with nuclear power, adult entertainment, gambling, alcohol, or investments in countries that violate human rights.

Some firms have made an effort to go beyond traditional negative screens and develop "positive" environmental, social, and governance criteria. The theory is that a company's ability to manage these risks correlates to its competitiveness, profitability, and share price performance. For example, the *Dow Jones Sustainability Index* is based on a variety of economic, environmental, and social criteria: climate change strategies, energy consumption, human resources development, knowledge management, stakeholder relations, and corporate governance, among others. Still, the majority of ESG indicators are qualitative (for example, "Does Company

X conduct an employee survey?"), and not directly correlated to financial performance. Goldman Sachs has integrated ESG data into its GS Sustain Index, which incorporates corporate governance; social issues with regard to leadership, employees, and wider stakeholders; and environmental management. In a description of GS Sustain, Goldman Sachs wrote, "We believe that it [ESG] is a good overall proxy for the management quality of companies relative to their peers and, as such, gives insight as to their ability to succeed on a sustainable basis."[4] A good overall proxy for management quality—that's about as far as the current generation of SRI analytics will get you.

Still, SRI has played an effective role in holding companies accountable to prescribed standards of conduct, marshaling the collective power of media, consumers, activists, and socially conscious investors. And it is largely due to the success of these social contract players that the capital markets have taken notice of corporate social performance. But in the brave new world of the social capital marketplace, the real inconvenient truth is that managing risk is not a sustainable investment philosophy; it is at best an input.

Mainstream capital is attracted to the social capital market because it believes that corporate social strategy offers companies a competitive business advantage. These next-generation SRI investors are looking for real social impact and real business value. ESG won't cut it. Basil Demeroutis, a senior partner at Capricorn Investment Group (a multi-billion-dollar investment firm that counts as its investors socially conscious luminaries like eBay cofounder Jeff Skoll and former Vice President Al Gore), describes the new investment mind-set this way: "It's not about picking a company that's going to do marginally less bad or a company that makes you feel good because it has a higher purpose. We are looking for *innovative* companies that are going to be at the forefront of tomorrow's business world *because* they are social change agents. The future predictor of business growth and success is not picking the right macro factors or social theme or opportunity—it's picking the companies that know how to leverage social change to effect business value."[5]

To meet this threshold, SRI will need to develop a new generation of data, and analytics, to measure corporate social innovation. These data will inform not only investment funds, but also next-generation corporate social rankings, market indexes, and analyst reports.

The Nonprofit Sector: Shift from Fundraising to "Selling Impact"

The social capital market will revolutionize the nonprofit sector— either that, or it will marginalize it. The outcome depends on how successfully nonprofits can adapt to a new allocation of capital and a new standard for value creation.

First off, nonprofits don't have the leverage they used to. Social change has become something of a commodity: with 1.4 million 501(c)(3) charities today, there is a lot of redundancy.[6] Interestingly, there are now approximately one thousand nonprofits for every type of social program, according to the Urban Institute.[7] Knowing this, nonprofits need to realize that in the SCM, social change is considered an investment, and corporate donors will be looking for a compelling return.

Second, psychic benefits are not enough of a return anymore. Corporate partners are looking to nonprofits to help drive business growth, not just make them feel better. That means nonprofits will need to master social innovation strategies and to find new, more meaningful ways of working with the private sector. To be effective, nonprofits will need to understand what is going on in the corporate world. It's important to know your "customer": how is the company doing financially, where do they operate, what are their key strategic priorities, and what social challenges do they face?

Nonprofits will need to approach companies differently— through the front door rather than the back door. In other words, rather than asking for a contribution as a charitable proposition, nonprofits need to figure out how to sell their impact as a business proposition. Social innovation offers many possibilities. To do this effectively, nonprofits must better inventory their assets, and they must be able to identify the social or business outcomes that they can deliver.

Finally, now more than ever, nonprofits have to deliver measurable results. It's not enough to show that the money was well spent—or at least not wasted. Nonprofits must be able to quantify and measure their outcomes to clearly demonstrate the value they are returning to corporate partners. Remember, corporate strategies are being evaluated internally on their ability to deliver results too, and they need to be able to rely on the data from their nonprofit partners to make that case.

Government: Shift from Programs to "Purchasing Results"

Despite the unprecedented surge in public spending on social programs, government is likely to become an increasingly marginal player in the social capital marketplace. First, with federal and state deficits soaring to historic levels, government spending will not likely be sustained (or repeated on this order of magnitude for many years to come). Currently, the federal budget is projected to show a deficit of $1.35 trillion for fiscal year 2010. At least forty-eight states addressed or still face shortfalls totaling $196 billion or 29 percent of state budgets for fiscal year 2010—the largest gaps on record.[8] But government isn't just broke—most Americans think it's broken (86 percent of Americans surveyed by CNN agreed).[9] To stay relevant with no money and no confidence, government will need to rely more on its bully pulpit and regulatory powers (versus taxing) and work more closely with private sector partners to effect social change (versus funding social programs).

There are many important social impacts that cannot easily be achieved through the social capital market (racism, youth violence, institution building, and civic participation, to name a few). Robert Reich, in his book *SuperCapitalism*, focuses on the limitations of corporate involvement in social change. He points out that "corporations are unfit to decide what is socially virtuous" (particularly on wedge issues like gay rights, abortion, and guns), and also "unable to deliver services that are inherently public."[10] It will make sense for government to shift its resources toward these high-value, lower-cost types of systemic changes and leverage the social capital market for what it can deliver best. Policymakers can also leverage government's "soft" powers to engage corporations and nonprofits in pursuit of public policy goals, much as I've described in Chapter Eight, Influence Policy Through Reverse Lobbying.

Government must also learn, much like the nonprofit sector, how to more effectively engage corporations in social change. I noted earlier in the book the growing government interest in PPPs (public-private partnerships). The federal government has already developed hundreds of PPPs with world-class companies and is just now beginning the process of evaluating which ones are effective and which ones aren't. Policymakers are also realizing that many of these PPPs are being conducted through the "back door" of companies' CSR and philanthropy departments, thereby limiting the resources invested and scope of business involvement (what one official called "getting a check and a logo"). Instead of this approach, government should consider going through the front door and working more directly with the "business" to create more significant social and business value. Social innovation strategies offer such an opportunity.

These are just a few of the implications of the social capital market. There are many more—for consumers, business partners, MBA students, academics, social activists, and philanthropists. For now, I will leave those to your analysis and imagination. I encourage you to debate these points, apply the concepts of this book to your work environments and classrooms, and come up with your own insights about the possibilities—and limitations—of social innovation for improving society and business performance.

Not Just Changing the World, But Making It Spin a Little Faster ...

We are living in a profound, strategic moment. The world has never before faced greater social ills—poverty, hunger, home-lessness, disease, lack of education, poor health care, threats to biodiversity—the list is overwhelming. At the same time, business has never before been so empowered to solve these problems—our wealth, ingenuity, technology, research, public consciousness, and market incentives have never been more abundant. What has been so confounding is that we have failed to find the right way to combine these vectors. Social innovation offers us that solution.

The simple truth is that corporations don't have a conscience; only people do. If we want to motivate business to solve social problems, we have to start from the assumption that companies will only ever care about the bottom line. We can critique that, bemoan it, rail against it, or try to change it. But we must also accept it—and find creative ways to inject social change into the stream of commerce, to work in concert with market forces. It is only in this way that we can unleash the full potential and resources of business to solve social problems. Social innovation taps into the engine of the market (economic growth and profit) rather than the fumes (charity and compliance). The five strategies I share in this book are only the beginning—there are many more yet to be discovered.

Let me also be clear about one thing: in writing this book and promoting these strategies, I am not endorsing any of these companies or suggesting that they are perfect. No company is. Some have been criticized for policies or practices that harm society or negatively impact the environment, and for those practices they should be held accountable. But we cannot afford to write off big business because we don't agree with everything it does. The opportunity cost to society is simply too great.

In fact, by focusing most of our energy on policing bad behavior and congratulating companies when they comply with standards, we may have set the bar too low. *Social Innovation, Inc.* shows that we can do so much more, and in a way that makes sense for business. It's time for entrepreneurs, CEOs, social change-makers, public officials, conscious consumers, employees, academics, philanthropists, and activists to focus on making business part of the solution.

Notes

Introduction

1. "Wal-Mart Supports Communities Around the Globe with $423 Million in Charitable Contributions." CSR press release, April 2, 2009. http://www.csrwire.com/press/press_release/ 24259-Wal-Mart-Supports-Communities-around-the-Globe-with-423-Million-in-Charitable-Contributions.

2. Wal-Mart Stores, Inc. "What to Know About Wal-Mart's $4 Prescription Program." Fact Sheet, May 2009. walmart-stores.com/download/2756.pdf. (Accessed March 30, 2010.)

3. "Wal-Mart $4 Generic Drug Program Available in All U.S. Stores Tomorrow." *Senior Journal*, November 27, 2006. http://seniorjournal.com/NEWS/MedicareDrugCards/6–11–27-Wal-Mart4GenericDrug.htm.

4. "Is Wal-Mart Too Powerful?" *BusinessWeek*, October 6, 2003. http://www.businessweek.com/magazine/content/03_40/ b3852001_mz001.htm.

5. Burritt, C., and Wolf, C. "Wal-Mart's Retail Muscle Helps Expand Drug Sales." *Bloomberg,* March 26, 2009. http://www.bloomberg.com/apps/news?pid=20601087&sid= a_2EHTz88F74.

6. Mendonca, L. T., and Oppenheim, J. M. "Investing in Sustainability: An Interview with Al Gore and David Blood." *McKinsey Quarterly*, May 2007.

Chapter One

1. Immelt, J. Plenary address presented at Business for Social Responsibility Conference, "Sustainability: Leadership Required." New York, November 2008.

2. "Siemens Expects 25 Billion Euro in Green-Product Sales by 2011." Sustainable Life Media, June 24, 2008. http://www.sustainablelifemedia.com/content/story/strategy/siemens_expects_25_billion_euro_in_green_product_sales.

3. Zolli, A. "Business 3.0." Fast Company, March 1, 2007. http://www.fastcompany.com/magazine/113/open_fast50-essay.html?page=0%2C3. (Accessed November 28, 2009.)

4. According to Corporate Responsibility Officer. http://www.thecro.com/files/CROMedia%20Kit2009_MB.pdf. December 4, 2008. (Accessed February 22, 2010.) Explanation provided by Jay Whitehead, president and publisher of CRO magazine, based on personal interview with Jason Saul, conducted February 22, 2010: "[T]his figure represents total spent on Corporate Responsibility, which includes environmental sustainability, governance, risk, compliance, social responsibility, and philanthropy; it was calculated by adding up the fees charged by about 450 service providers and 100 NGOs for sustainability, CSR, and philanthropy-related services and technologies in the U.S., Canada, and Western Europe."

5. "GE's 2008 Ecomagination Revenues to Rise 21%, Cross $17 Billion." General Electric press release, October 21, 2008.

6. "European SRI Study 2008." Eurosif, October 2008. http://www.eurosif.org/publications/sri_studies.

7. "Socially Responsible Investing Facts." Social Investment Forum. http://www.socialinvest.org/resources/sriguide/srifacts.cfm.

8. Ibid.

9. Ibid.

10. "European SRI Study 2008." *Eurosif*, October 2008. http://www.eurosif.org/publications/sri_studies.

11. "Dow Jones Sustainability World Index, October 2009." Dow Jones Sustainability Indexes, 2009. http://www.sustainability-index.com/djsi_pdf/publications/Factsheets/SAM_Indexes Monthly_DJSIWorld.pdf. (Accessed May 17, 2010.)

12. Goldman Sachs. "Introducing GS SUSTAIN." June 22, 2007. www.unglobalcompact.org/docs/summit2007/gs_esg_embargoed_until030707pdf.pdf. (Accessed February 27, 2010.)

13. Banjo, S. "New Investing Standards Coming for Microfinance." *Wall Street Journal Blogs*, September 25, 2009. http://blogs.wsj.com/financial-adviser/2009/09/25/new-investing-standards-coming-for-microfinance/.

14. Gates, B. "Making Capitalism More Creative." *Time*, July 31, 2008. http://www.time.com/time/business/article/0,8599,1828069-2,00.html#ixzz0g0KDXH8o.

15. Schlosser, E. *Fast Food Nation: The Dark Side of the All-American Meal.* New York: Houghton Mifflin, 2002. Excerpted in http://www.nytimes.com/books/first/s/schlosser-fast.html.

16. Ibid.

17. Anderson, S., and Cavanagh, J. "The Rise of Corporate Global Power." Institute for Policy Studies, December 4, 2000.

18. Chu, J. "Infographic: Count: Really Big Business." *Fast Company*, no. 131, December 10, 2008.

19. Wong, G. "Fortune 500: Shakeup at the Top." *CNN-Money.com*, April 3, 2006. http://money.cnn.com/2006/03/31/news/companies/top25_f500_fortune/index.htm.

20. "Al Gore's Fund to Close After Attracting $5 Billion." *New York Times*, March 11, 2008.

21. Bonini, S.M.J., McKillop, K., and Mendonca, L. T. "The Trust Gap Between Consumers and Corporations." *McKinsey*

Quarterly, May 2007. https://www.mckinseyquarterly.com/
The_trust_gap_between_consumers_and_corporations_1985.

22. Ibid.

23. "MTV Networks in Asia & Pacific and MTV Europe Foundation Launch Youth-Focused Anti-Human Trafficking Campaign." Humantrafficking.org, August 12, 2007. http://www.humantrafficking.org/updates/690.

24. Zolli, A. "Business 3.0." *Fast Company*, March 1, 2007. http://www.fastcompany.com/magazine/113/open_fast50-essay.html?page=0%2C3. (Accessed November 28, 2009.) Subsequent information in paragraph is also from this source.

25. Bielak, G., Bonini, S.M.J., and Oppenheim, J. M. "CEOs on Strategy and Social Issues." *McKinsey Quarterly*, October 2007. https://www.mckinseyquarterly.com/article_print.aspx?L2=33&L3=117&ar=2056.

26. Parfit, M. "Future Power: Where Will the World Get Its Next Energy Fix?" *National Geographic*, August 2005. http://ngm.nationalgeographic.com/ngm/0508/feature1/fulltext.html. (Accessed November 29, 2009.)

27. General Electric. "Ecomagination." http://ge.ecomagination.com/.

28. "Fast Facts." National Center for Education Statistics. http://nces.ed.gov/fastfacts/display.asp?id=16. (Accessed February 13, 2010.)

29. Education Industry Association. "Overview of the Education Industry Association." http://www.educationindustry.org/tier.asp?sid=1.

30. Ibid.

31. "Health Care Trends." Plunkett Research, 2009. http://www.plunkettresearch.com/Industries/HealthCare/HealthCareTrends/tabid/294/Default.aspx.

32. Ibid.

33. Saad, L. "Cost Is Foremost Healthcare Issue for Americans." *Gallup*, September 23, 2009. http://www.gallup.com/poll/123149/cost-is-foremost-healthcare-issue-for-americans.aspx.

34. Gates, B. "Making Capitalism More Creative." *Time*, July 31, 2008. http://www.time.com/time/business/article/0,8599,1828069-2,00.html#ixzz0g0KDXH8o.

35. Engardio, P. "Beyond the Green Corporation: Moving Away from Platitudes to Strategies That Help World and Bottom Line." *BusinessWeek*, January 19, 2007.

36. "Change in Corporate Foundation Giving and Assets, 1987 to 2007." FC Stats: The Foundation Center's Statistical Information Service, 2009. http://foundationcenter.org/findfunders/statistics/pdf/02_found_growth/2007/01_07.pdf.

37. "FC Stats: Grantmaker Information." The Foundation Center, 2010. http://foundationcenter.org/findfunders/statistics/grantmakerinfo.html.

38. Whelan, D., Serafin, T., and von Zeppelin, C. "Billion-Dollar Donors." *Forbes*, August 24, 2009. http://www.forbes.com/2009/08/24/billion-dollar-donors-gates-business-billionaire-philanthropy.html.

39. Low, J., and Kalafut, P. C. *Invisible Advantage: How Intangibles Are Driving Business Performance*. New York: Cap Gemini Ernst & Young, 2002.

40. Chatzkel, J. "A Conversation with Jon Low." *Journal of Intellectual Capital*, 2001, 2(2), 136–147. See also Chabrow, E., and Colkin, E., "Hidden Value." *Information Week Global CIO*, April 22, 2002. http://www.informationweek.com/news/global-cio/showArticle.jhtml?articleID=6501923. (Accessed February 19, 2010.)

41. Lubber, M. "Is ESG Data Going Mainstream?" *Harvard Business Review Blogs: Leading Green*, May 6, 2009.

http://blogs.harvardbusiness.org/leadinggreen/2009/05/is-esg-data-going-mainstream.html. (Accessed December 1, 2009.)

Chapter Two

1. Gap Inc. "Gap (PRODUCT)REDTM." http://www.gapinc.com/red.
2. The Avon Foundation. "Avon Breast Cancer Crusade – Homepage." http://www.avoncompany.com/women/avoncrusade/.
3. Mendelsohn, S. "Green Olympic Sponsors: Coca-Cola ... Going Blue?" July 18, 2008. http://responsiblechina.com/2008/07/18/blue-olymic-sponors-coca-cola/.
4. Engardio, P. "Beyond the Green Corporation: Moving Away from Platitudes to Strategies That Help World and Bottom Line." *BusinessWeek*, January 19, 2007.
5. Corporate Responsibility Officer. "Member Benefits," December 4, 2008. http://www.thecro.com/files/CROMedia%20Kit2009_MB.pdf. (Accessed February 22, 2010.) The figure represents the total spent on corporate responsibility, which includes environmental sustainability, governance, risk, compliance, social responsibility, and philanthropy; it was calculated by adding up the fees charged by about 450 service providers and 100 NGOs for sustainability, CSR, and philanthropy-related services and technologies in the United States, Canada, and Western Europe.
6. Coady, M. "Giving in Numbers: 2007 Edition." Committee Encouraging Corporate Philanthropy. www.corporatephilanthropy.org/resources/benchmarking-reports/giving-in-numbers.html.
7. Ibid.
8. Schwartz, M., and Lubliner, P. "Getting Gas." *GOOD.is/Marketplace*, December 11, 2006. http://www.good.is/post/getting-gas. (Accessed February 21, 2010.)

9. "Just Good Business." *Economist*, January 19, 2008, 386(8563), 3–6.

10. Berger, I. E., Drumwright, M. E., and Cunningham, P. "Mainstreaming Corporate Social Responsibility: Developing Markets for Virtue." *California Management Review*, 2007, 49(4), 132–157.

11. McDonald's. "Good Works Overview." http://www.mcdonalds .com/usa/good/overview_new.html. (Accessed February 22, 2010.)

12. McDonald's. "2009 CR Report: A Filet-o-Fish We Can All Feel Good About." 2009. http://aboutmcdonalds .com/mcd/csr/report/sustainable_supply_chain/resource_ conservation/sustainable_fisheries.html.

13. McDonald's. "2009 CR Report: Doing the Right Thing Is Important to Us." 2009. http://aboutmcdonalds.com/mcd/ csr/report/overview.html.

14. "Who's Socially Responsible?" *Fortune Talkback, CNN-Money.com*, October 20, 2006. money.cnn.com/blogs/ talkback/2006_10_20_archive.html.

15. "AccountAbility 1000 (AA1000) Framework: Standards, Guidelines and Professional Qualification." The Institute of Social and Ethical AccountAbility. Exposure Draft, November 1999, p. 2.

16. "The Global Reporting Initiative." March 2010. www .globalreporting.org. See also AccountAbility, "AA1000 Series of Standards," 2007. www.accountability21.com/ aa1000series.

17. "KPMG International Survey of Corporate Responsibility Reporting 2005." KPMG Global Sustainability Services, June 2005. http://www.kpmg.com.au/Portals/0/KPMG%20Survey% 202005_3.pdf.

18. Leibs, S. "Sustainability Reporting: Earth in the Balance Sheet." *CFO Magazine*, December 1, 2007. http://www.cfo .com/printable/article.cfm/10234097.

19. Vogel, D. *The Market for Virtue: The Potential and Limits of Corporate Social Responsibility*. Washington, D.C.: Brookings Institution Press, 2005, p. 17.

20. Porter, M. E., and Kramer, M. R. "Strategy & Society: The Link Between Competitive Advantage and Corporate Social Responsibility." *Harvard Business Review*, December 2006.

21. Ibid.

22. "Giving in Numbers: 2008 Edition." Committee Encouraging Corporate Philanthropy, 2008. http://www.corporate philanthropy.org/pdfs/giving_in_numbers/GivinginNumbers 2008.pdf.

23. Glasser, J. "Dark Cloud: Ben & Jerry's Inaccurate in Rainforest Nut Pitch." *Boston Globe*, July 30, 1995.

24. Ibid.

Chapter Three

1. Walton, S. *Sam Walton: Made in America*. New York: Bantam Books, 1993, pp. 306–307.

2. Schoenberger, K. *Levi's Children*. New York: Grove Press, 2001.

3. Austin, J., and Reficco, E. "Corporate Social Entrepreneurship." Working Paper 09–101. Harvard Business School, 2009.

4. Ibid.

5. Gates, B. "Making Capitalism More Creative." *Time*, July 31, 2008. http://www.time.com/time/business/article/0,8599, 1828069-2,00.html#ixzz0gOKDXH8o.

6. Cummings, L. "Facts About Aluminum Recycling." Earth911.com, April 2, 2007. http://earth911.com/blog/2007/ 04/02/facts-about-aluminum-recycling/.

7. Cummins Inc. "Cummins News." http://www.cummins.com/ cmi/content.jsp?dataId=2937&anchorId=1814&menuIndex =0&siteId=1&overviewId=15&menuId=4&langId=1033&.

8. Jean S. Blackwell, executive vice president of corporate responsibility and chief executive of the Cummins Foundation, Cummins Inc., personal interview with Jason Saul, February 18, 2010.

9. Gaynor, T. "Tesco Launch Stirs High Hopes in U.S. 'Food Deserts.'" *Reuters*, August 22, 2007. http://www.reuters.com/ article/idUSN2128683620070822. (Accessed February 23, 2010.)

10. Wrigley, N., Warm, D., Margetts, B., and Whelan, A. "Assessing the Impact of Improved Retail Access on Diet in a 'Food Desert': A Preliminary Report." *Urban Studies*, 2002, 39(11), 2061–2082.

11. GE *ecomagination* website. http://ge.ecomagination.com/ products/waste-to-value.html.

12. Smith, A. *An Inquiry into the Nature and Causes of the Wealth of Nations*, Volume I, 1776, Chapter 2, paragraph 2 (available online at http://oll.libertyfund.org/220/111839/2312795).

13. Gates, B. Harvard commencement remarks, June 6, 2007. http://www.gatesfoundation.org/speeches-commentary/Pages/ bill-gates-2007-harvard-commencement.aspx.

14. Christensen, C. M., Baumann, H., Ruggles, R., and Sadtler, T. M. "Disruptive Innovation for Social Change." *Harvard Business Review*, December 2006.

15. The term "sustainability" is broadly about "meeting humanity's needs without harming future generations." (See Engardio, P. "Beyond the Green Corporation: Moving Away from Platitudes to Strategies That Help World and Bottom Line," *BusinessWeek*, January 19, 2007.) This can apply to economic

development, the environment, and other areas; here I'm focusing on its environment-related meaning.

16. "Q + A." The Breakthrough Institute. http://www .thebreakthrough.org/QnA.shtml. (Accessed February 25, 2010.)

17. Gunther, M. "The Green Machine." *Fortune*, July 31, 2006.

18. Gogoi, P. "What's with Wal-Mart's Sales Woes?" *Business-Week*, November 29, 2006.

19. Scott, H. L. "Twenty-First Century Leadership." Presented on October 24, 2005. http://walmartwatch.com/img/documents/ 21st_Century_Leadership.pdf.

20. Plambeck, E. L., and Denend, L. "The Greening of Wal-Mart." *Stanford Social Innovation Review*, 2008, 6(2), 53–59. http://www.ssireview.org/articles/entry/the_greening_of_wal_ mart/. (Accessed February 25, 2010.)

21. "Q + A." The Breakthrough Institute. http://www .thebreakthrough.org/QnA.shtml. (Accessed February 25, 2010.)

22. Engardio, "Beyond the Green Corporation."

23. "Corporate Citizenship: Profiting from a Sustainable Business." *Economist Intelligence Unit*, 2008.

24. Ibid.

25. Engardio, "Beyond the Green Corporation."

Chapter Four

1. Gurel, O. "Innovation vs. Invention: Knowing the Difference Makes a Difference." Wisconsin Technology Network, September 18, 2007. http://wistechnology.com/articles/4184/.

2. See also Smith, S., "'Young Invincibles' OK with Risk of No Insurance," *CNNhealth.com*, March 20, 2009. http://www.cnn.com/2009/HEALTH/03/20/catastrophic

.insurance.invincibles/index.html#cnnSTCText. For the sixth consecutive year, the number of Americans living without health insurance has risen, according to new U.S. Census Bureau data. Approximately 2.2 million people were added to the "uninsurance" rolls in 2006—the largest one-year increase in five years. Annual Census Bureau estimates showed 47 million people, or 15.8 percent of the U.S. population, were without health insurance during 2006—a 4.9 percent increase. Most of the research shows that most uninsured are "poor." That's true: 36 percent of the uninsured have incomes below the poverty level ($20,614 for a family of four). But many of the "poor" are young adults. According to the Urban Institute, almost half of uninsured young adults make less than $14,000 a year. And according to the Commonwealth Fund, the difficult nature of obtaining and keeping health insurance coverage in entry-level jobs has resulted in major increases in the numbers of uninsured younger adults ages 25–34 and uninsured older adults ages 45–64. See: Johnson, T. D. "Census Bureau: Number of U.S. Uninsured Rises to 47 Million Americans Are Uninsured: Almost 5 Percent Increase Since 2005." *Nation's Health*, 2007, 37(8). http://www.medscape.com/viewarticle/567737. Moreover, close to 4 in 10 Americans (38%)—by far the largest percentage mentioned for any issue—cite the cost or affordability of health care as the nation's biggest health care problem. And 72 percent of the uninsured say costs are a major problem. See: Saad, L. "Cost Is Foremost Healthcare Issue for Americans." *Gallup*, September 23, 2009. http://www.gallup.com/poll/123149/cost-is-foremost-healthcare-issue-for-americans.aspx.

3. Kriss, J. L., Collins, S. R., Mahato, B., Gould, E., and Schoen, C. "Rite of Passage? Why Young Adults Become Uninsured and How New Policies Can Help, 2008 Update." The Commonwealth Fund, May 30, 2008. http://www

.commonwealthfund.org/~/media/Files/Publications/Issue%
20Brief/2009/Aug/1310_Nicholson_rite_of_passage_2009.pdf.

4. Mary Floyd, vice president, individual sales, WellPoint, and Jerry Slowey, director of public relations, WellPoint, personal interviews with Jason Saul, November 12, 2009.

5. Ibid.

6. Ibid.

7. Weber, J. "Making Health Insurance Hip: WellPoint See Growth Selling No-Frills Coverage to Twentysome-things." *BusinessWeek*. http://www.businessweek.com/ magazine/content/07_12/b4026084.htm. March 19, 2007.

8. Ibid.

9. Ibid.

10. Prahalad, C. K., and Hart, S. "Strategies for the Bottom of the Pyramid: Creating Sustainable Development." Ann Arbor: University of Michigan Business School, August 1999. http://www.nd.edu/~kmatta/mgt648/strategies.pdf.

11. Anderson, C. "About Me." http://thelongtail.com/about.html.

12. Anderson, C. "Long Tail vs. Bottom of Pyramid." *The Long Tail—Chris Anderson's Blog*. March 22, 2005. http://longtail .typepad.com/the_long_tail/2005/03/long_tail_vs_bo.html.

13. Prahalad and Hart, "Strategies for the Bottom of the Pyramid."

14. Engardio, "Beyond the Green Corporation."

15. Bower, J. L., and Christensen, C. M. "Disruptive Technologies: Catching the Wave." *Harvard Business Review*, 73(1), January-February 1995, 43–53.

16. Ibid.

17. Christensen, C. M., Baumann, H., Ruggles, R., and Sadtler, T. M. "Disruptive Innovation for Social Change." *Harvard Business Review*, December 2006.

18. Ibid.

19. Ibid.

20. Letelier, M. F., Flores, F., and Spinosa, C. "Developing Productive Customers in Emerging Markets." *California Management Review*, 2003, 45(4), 77–103.

21. Hannah, D. C. "Want to Reach a Trillion-Dollar Market? Don't Ignore People with Disabilities." Diversity Inc., October 28, 2008, citing the U.S. Census Bureau. www.diversityinc .com/content/1757/article/4477.

22. Ibid. Citing the U.S. Census Bureau, 2000; Witeck-Combs Communications/Harris Interactive poll, 2005; The National Organization on Disability/Harris Interactive poll of Americans with Disabilities, 2004.

23. Ibid. Citing the Travel Industry Association of America/Harris Interactive/Open Doors/Society for Accessible Travel and Hospitality Survey, 2002; The National Organization on Disability/Harris Interactive poll of Americans with Disabilities, 2004.

24. Floyd and Slowey interviews (see note 4).

25. Floyd and Slowey interviews. See also Cass, J., "Are You Looking for a Tonik?" *PR Communications*. http://pr.typepad .com/pr_communications/2006/06/are_you_looking.html.

26. Day, K. "Wal-Mart to Sell 300 Drugs for $4." *Seattle Times*, September 22, 2006.

27. "Wal-Mart $4 Generic Drug Program Available in All U.S. Stores Tomorrow." *Senior Journal*, November 27, 2006. http://seniorjournal.com/NEWS/MedicareDrugCards/6–11– 27-Wal-Mart4GenericDrug.htm.

28. Ibid.

29. Jana, R. "Innovation Trickles in a New Direction." *Business-Week*, March 11, 2009.

30. U.S. Food and Drug Administration. "Generic Drugs: What You Need to Know." Office of Generic Drugs, Center for Drug Evaluation and Research, April 30, 2009. http://www.fda .gov/drugs/emergencypreparedness/bioterrorismanddrug preparedness/ucm134451.htm.

31. Ibid.

32. Jana, "Innovation."

33. GE *healthymagination* website. http://www.ge.com/innovation/ healthymagination/index.html. (Accessed March 22, 2010.)

34. Arvind Gopalratnam, spokesman, GE Healthcare, personal interview with Jason Saul via e-mail, November 16, 2009.

35. Ibid.

36. Ibid.

37. Brewer, J. "Nonprofit Innovation with Salesforce.com." *Huffington Post*, February 14, 2008. http://www.huffingtonpost .com/jake-brewer/nonprofit-innovation-with_b_86723.html.

38. Jana, "Innovation."

39. Immelt, J. Plenary address. Presented at Business for Social Responsibility Conference "Sustainability: Leadership Required." New York, November 2008. Summary available at http://www.bsr.org/ClientFiles/BAS/Conference2008/ Materials/BSR_Conf2008_GE_Plenary.pdf, and video available at http://www.ge.com/audio_video/ge/jeff_immelt/ immelt_talks_about_sustainability_at_the_bsr_conference .html.

40. Barbaro, M., and Abelson, R. "Relief for Some But Maybe Not Many in Wal-Mart Plan for $4 Generic Drugs." *New York Times*, September 22, 2006.

41. U.S. Food and Drug Administration. "Generic Drugs: What You Need to Know." Office of Generic Drugs, Center for Drug Evaluation and Research, April 30, 2009.

42. Jana, "Innovation."

Chapter Five

1. Gaynor, T. "Tesco Launch Stirs High Hopes in U.S. 'Food Deserts.'" *Reuters*, August 22, 2007. http://www.reuters .com/article/idUSN2128683620070822. (Accessed February 25, 2010.)

2. Misonzhnik, E. "UK Giant Tesco Tiptoes Into U.S. Supermarket Wars." *Retail Traffic*, September 28, 2006. http://retailtrafficmag.com/retailing/tesco_tiptoes_ supermarket/.

3. "TESCO PLC – Interim Results 2009/10." Tesco press release, October 6, 2009. http://www.tescocorporate.com/plc/ir/pres_ results/results/r2010/InterimResults09_10/pressrelease_ interims2009_10.pdf. (Accessed February 25, 2010.)

4. Ibid.

5. Gaynor, "Tesco Launch Stirs High Hopes."

6. Wood, Z. "Tesco Puts the Cart Before the Trolley in the Bid to Crack America." *Observer*, June 10, 2007. http://www.guardian .co.uk/business/2007/jun/10/supermarkets.retail1. (Accessed February 25, 2010.)

7. The White House. "First Lady Michelle Obama Launches Let's Move: America's Move to Raise a Healthier Generation of Kids." Office of the First Lady, February 9, 2010. http://www.whitehouse.gov/the-press-office/first-lady-michelle-obama-launches-lets-move-americas-move-raise-a-healthier-genera. (Accessed February 25, 2010.)

8. Wrigley, N., Warm, D., and Margetts, B. "Deprivation, Diet and Food Retail Access: Findings from the Leeds 'Food Deserts' Study." *Environment and Planning A*, 35(1), 2003, 151–188.

9. Shaffer, A., and Gottlieb, R. "Filling in 'Food Deserts.'" *Los Angeles Times*, November 5, 2007. (Accessed February 25, 2010.)

10. Coca-Cola Company. "Supporting Small Business Development." http://www.thecoca-colacompany.com/citizenship/community_case_studies.html. (Accessed February 25, 2010.)

11. Coca-Cola Company. "Micro-Distribution Models in Africa: Coca-Cola's Manual Distribution System," April 21, 2009. http://api.ning.com/files/mmVoOE-YKk95aDcnvUmnHqy HbPZsEdqalb1DeTSK22ThTY8q3QdIFViIVZCDZ68Ne2ZJw 4OiaNQLx9Lw4jadhrNioF474NV-/MDCPres21April09.pdf. (Accessed February 8, 2010.)

12. Nelson, J., Ishikawa, E., and Geaneotes, A. "Developing Inclusive Business Models: A Review of Coca-Cola's Manual Distribution Centers in Ethiopia and Tanzania." Harvard Kennedy School and International Finance Corporation, 2009. http://www.hks.harvard.edu/m-rcbg/CSRI/publications/other_10_MDC_report.pdf. (Accessed February 25, 2010.)

13. Ibid.

14. Coca-Cola, "Supporting Small Business Development."

15. Nelson, Ishikawa, and Geaneotes, "Developing Inclusive Business Models." See also Coca-Cola, "Micro-Distribution Models in Africa."

16. Hamm, S. "Coke: On Doing Well by Doing Good." Business-Week, May 13, 2009. http://www.businessweek.com/globalbiz/blog/globespotting/archives/2009/05/coke_on_doing_w.html. (Accessed February 25, 2010.)

17. Porter, M. E. "The Rise of the Urban Entrepreneur." Inc., May 15, 1995.

18. Broder, J. M. "Clinton, in Poverty Tour, Focuses on Profits." New York Times, July 7, 1999, p. A14.

19. The White House, "First Lady Michelle Obama Launches Let's Move."

20. Ibid.

21. Schuette, D. "Ambassador Elizabeth Bagley Talks About Partnership with Private Sector." *VOANews.com*, November 16, 2009. http://www1.voanews.com/english/news/a-13-2009-11-16-voa33-70423962.html. (Accessed February 8, 2010.)

22. Ibid.

23. Clinton Global Initiative. "About Us." http://www.clinton globalinitiative.org/aboutus/default.asp?Section=AboutUs& PageTitle=About%20Us. (Accessed February 8, 2010.)

24. "The State of Corporate Philanthropy: A McKinsey Global Survey." *McKinsey Quarterly*, February 2008. http://www .mckinseyquarterly.com/Corporate_Finance/Valuation/ The_state_of_corporate_philanthropy_A_McKinsey_Global_ Survey_2106. (Accessed February 25, 2010.)

25. Ball, J. "Digging Deep: As Exxon Pursues African Oil, Charity Becomes a Political Issue." *Wall Street Journal*, January 10, 2006. Examples in paragraph are from this source.

26. Ibid.

27. "The Conference Board: Economic Downturn Will Have Major Effects on Corporate Philanthropy in 2009." *Fundraising Success*, March 3, 2009. http://www.fundraisingsuccessmag .com/article/the-conference-board-economic-downturn-will-have-major-effects-corporate-philanthropy-2009-403938/1. (Accessed February 25, 2010.)

28. Ball, "Digging Deep."

29. Wood, "Tesco Puts the Cart Before the Trolley" (see chap. 5, n. 5).

30. Coca-Cola, "Micro-Distribution Models in Africa."

31. "India: Creating Rural Entrepreneurs." Unilever. http://www.unilever.com/sustainability/casestudies/economic-development/creating-rural-entrepreneurs.aspx. (Accessed February 25, 2010.)

32. Cescau, P. "Beyond Corporate Responsibility: Social Innovation and Sustainable Development as Drivers of Business Growth." Presented at INDEVOR Alumni Forum, France, May 25, 2007. http://www.unilever.com/Images/ Beyond%20Corporate%20Responsibilty%20-%20Social %20innovation%20and%20sustainable%20development %20as%20drivers%20of%20business%20growth_tcm13- 95521.pdf. (Accessed February 25, 2010.)

33. "Colalife: About." Colalife. http://www.colalife.org/about/. (Accessed February 25, 2010.)

34. Seth Starner, senior business innovations manager, Amway, personal interview with Jason Saul, January 27, 2010.

35. "Retail Memo: Tesco Fresh & Easy Insight: A New Store Blooms in Compton, CA.; F&E's Chicagoland March; a Sacramento Neighborhood and F&E Get Hitched." Natural~Specialty Foods Memo: News, Analysis, Insight and Opinion, February 8, 2008. http://naturalspecialtyfoodsmemo .blogspot.com/2008/02/retail-memo-tesco-fresh-easy-day-new .html. (Accessed February 25, 2010.)

36. Ibid.

37. "Lifebuoy Spreads Hygiene Message to Millions of Children in 23 Countries on 15 October 2008—The First Ever Global Handwashing Day." Lifebuoy. http://www.lifebuoy .com/downloads/news/08sepglobalhandwashingday_2.pdf. (Accessed February 25, 2010.)

38. Ibid.

39. Ibid.

40. Katie Carroll, secretariat coordinator, Global Public-Private Partnership for Handwashing, personal interview with Jason Saul via e-mail, March 30, 2010.

41. "Lifebuoy Spreads Hygiene Message."

42. Carroll interview, referencing information shared by Dr. Myriam Sidibe, Ph.D., Lifebuoy global social mission manager at Unilever.

43. Unilever. "Annual Report and Accounts 2009: Creating a Better Future Every Day." http://www.unilever.com/images/ ir_Unilever_AR09_tcm13–208066.pdf, p. 19.

44. Lifebuoy. "Way of Life: Towards Universal Handwashing with Soap: Annual Review 2008/09." http://www.unilever .com/images/sd_WayofLifeJan2010_for_web1_tcm13–212739 .pdf.

45. Butler, S. "Tesco's Fresh & Easy Stores Hit Image Problem Before Opening." *Times Online*, August 3, 2007. http://business .timesonline.co.uk/tol/business/industry_sectors/retailing/ article2189609.ece. (Accessed February 25, 2010.)

46. Ibid.

47. Ibid.

48. Coca-Cola Company. News release: "The Coca-Cola System Advances New Solutions for Economic Development," May 13, 2009. http://www.thecoca-colacompany.com/presscenter/ nr_20090513_kent_economic_development.html. (Accessed February 25, 2010.)

Chapter Six

1. According to a National Education Association Survey of over three million members, teachers annually spend $1,200 of their own money on average for much-needed learning resources beyond their schools' budgets. See "Today OfficeMax Surprises 1300 Teachers in Second Annual 'A Day Made Better' Nationwide Event." *PR Newswire*, October 1, 2008. http://investor.officemax.com/phoenix.zhtml?c=85171&p= irol-newsArticle&ID=1216309&highlight. (Accessed February 5, 2010.) This statistic is even more meaningful in

the context of the average teacher salary—about $30,000 per year; see "OfficeMax's 'A Day Made Better' Nationwide Cause Event." Video available at http://video.filestube .com/watch,1b1e891da35db57d03ea/OfficeMax-s-A-Day-Made-Better-Nationwide-Cause-Event.html. (Accessed February 6, 2010.)

2. Epstein-Reeves, J. "Leaders in the Field: A Day Made Better." *CitizenPolity*, September 29, 2009. http://citizenpolity .com/2009/09/29/leaders-in-the-field-a-day-made-better/. (Accessed February 5, 2010.) Also source of photo.

3. "Today OfficeMax Surprises 1300 Teachers in Second Annual 'A Day Made Better' Nationwide Event." *PR Newswire*, October 1, 2008. http://investor.officemax.com/ phoenix.zhtml?c=85171&p=irol-newsArticle&ID=1216309 &highlight. (Accessed February 5, 2010.)

4. Ibid.

5. Ibid.

6. William Bonner, senior director of external relations, OfficeMax, personal interview with Jason Saul, February 25, 2010.

7. Epstein-Reeves, "Leaders in the Field."

8. "OfficeMax 'Eve' Branding Training Video." http://www .youtube.com/watch?v=xHZh5W_sxo8. (Accessed February 6, 2010.)

9. Epstein-Reeves, "Leaders in the Field."

10. William Bonner interview.

11. James Epstein-Reeves, former community affairs director, OfficeMax, personal interview with Jason Saul, February 23, 2010.

12. James Epstein-Reeves interview; employee quotes from same source.

13. Approximately 17 percent of Walmart's measurable growth in traffic in early 2009 came from new customers, according to Walmart CEO Mike Duke. See: Duff, M. "Wal-Mart Focuses on Retaining Customers Beyond Recession." *bnet,* May 14, 2009. http://industry.bnet.com/retail/10001915/Wal-mart-focuses-on-retaining-customers-beyond-recession/.

14. McEwen, W. J. "Getting Emotional About Brands." *Gallup Management Journal,* September 9, 2004. http://gmj.gallup.com/content/12910/getting-emotional-about-brands.aspx.

15. IEG statistic reported in Wikipedia, "Cause Marketing." http://en.wikipedia.org/wiki/Cause_marketing. (Accessed November 29, 2009.)

16. Jennifer Smith, director of communications, Ronald McDonald House Charities Global Data, personal interview with Jason Saul, February 25, 2010.

17. Landau, E. "Obesity, Politics, STDs Flow in Social Networks." *CNN.com,* October 8, 2009. http://www.cnn.com/2009/TECH/10/08/social.networks.connected.

18. McEwen, "Getting Emotional About Brands."

19. Haque, U. "The Scale Every Business Needs." *Harvard Business Review* blogs, January 20, 2010. http://blogs.hbr.org/haque/2010/01/the_scale_every_business_needs.html.

20. Jayson, S. "Generation Y Gets Involved." *USA Today,* October 24, 2006. http://www.usatoday.com/news/nation/2006–10–23-gen-next-cover_x.htm.

21. Zolli, A. "Business 3.0." *Fast Company,* March 1, 2007. http://www.fastcompany.com/magazine/113/open_fast50-essay.html?page=0%2C3. (Accessed November 28, 2009.)

22. Stepanek, M. "Cause-Washing: The New Black?" Justmeans, March 11, 2010. http://www.justmeans.com/Cause-washing-new-black/10558.html.

23. Devinney, T. M., Auger, P., Eckhardt, G., and Birtchnell, T. "The Other CSR." *Stanford Social Innovation Review*, Fall 2006.

24. Grocery store statistics from: Schwartz, B. *Paradox of Choice: Why More Is Less.* New York: HarperCollins, 2004.

25. Pink, D. H. *A Whole New Mind.* New York: Penguin Group, 2006.

26. "Pampers® together with actress Salma Hayek helps UNICEF move closer toward goal of eliminating deadly Tetanus through global 'ONE PACK=ONE VACCINE' Campaign." Press release, February 5, 2009. http://www.unicefusa.org/news/releases/pampers-together-with-actress.html.

27. "Why Tetanus? Quick Facts." http://www.unicefusa.org/hidden/tetanus-quick-facts.html.

28. "Pampers® together with actress Salma Hayek" press release.

29. Bryan McCleary, P&G Baby Division, personal interview with Jason Saul, April 30, 2010.

30. "Mommy Bloggers and UNICEF Unite to Wipe Out Tetanus." lilsugar, August 13, 2008. http://www.lilsugar.com/Mommy-Bloggers-UNICEF-Unite-Wipe-Out-Tetanus-1863363.

31. Bonner interview (see chap. 6, n. 6).

32. "Climate Change Corp: Climate News for Business." http://www.climatechangecorp.com/content.asp?contentid=6178.

33. HSBC. "Sustainable Finance." http://www.hsbc.com/1/2/sustainability/sustainable-finance, and "Climate Change Corp: Climate News for Business."

34. Ibid.

35. "Climate Change Corp: Climate News for Business."

36. "Pampers & UNICEF Connect Moms Around the World." http://alphamom.com/your-life/pampers-unicef-connect-moms-around-the-world/.

Chapter Seven

1. Connecticut State Department of Education. *Report on Progress in the Hartford Public Schools*, June 1, 2005. http://www .sde.ct.gov/sde/lib/sde/PDF/Equity/hartford/Narrative_June05 .pdf.

2. Bordonaro, G. "Creating a New Generation of Workers: Business Community Key to City's Learning Academies." *Hartford Business Journal Online*, June 29, 2009. http://www.hartford business.com/news9364.html. (Accessed February 10, 2010.)

3. Marlene Ibsen, CEO, Travelers Foundation, personal interviews with Jason Saul, January 28, 2010, and March 26, 2010.

4. City of Hartford. "Steven Adamowski, Hartford's New Superintendent." http://www.hartford.gov/ofyc/Superintendent Adamowski.pdf. (Accessed February 10, 2010.)

5. Goode, S. "Hartford Shows Improvement in High School Graduation Rate." HartfordInfo.org, September 23, 2009. http://www.hartfordinfo.org/issues/documents/education/htfd _courant_092309.asp.

6. Hartford Public Schools. "Hartford Public Schools." http://www.hartfordschools.org/schools/Hartfords-Insurance-and-Finance-Academy.php. See also Bordonaro, "Creating a New Generation of Workers."

7. Bordonaro, "Creating a New Generation of Workers."

8. Ibid.

9. Ibid.

10. Ibid.

11. "IBM Collaborating with Hundreds of Universities Driving Curriculum Change for a Smarter Planet." IBM press release, April 13, 2009. http://www-03.ibm.com/press/us/en/ pressrelease/27201.wss. (Accessed March 23, 2010.)

12. Chaker, A. M. "Majoring in IBM: Dissatisfied with Graduates, Companies Design and Fund Curricula at Universities." *Wall Street Journal*, September 12, 2006.

13. "IBM Collaborating with Hundreds of Universities."

14. Chaker, "Majoring in IBM."

15. *Giving USA 2009: The Annual Report on Philanthropy for the Year 2008*. Indiana University: Giving USA Foundation, 2009. (Corporate philanthropy numbers are based on the 2008 *Corporate Contributions Report* by the Conference Board as cited on pages 72–73, and the Foundation Center's survey of foundation giving as cited on page 74.)

16. "Fast Forward: 25 Trends That Will Change the Way You Do Business." *Workforce*, June 2003, pp. 43–56. http://www.workforce.com/section/09/feature/23/45/53/index.html.

17. Meghan Tallent-Bennis, former manager, Strategy and Planning, Office of Teaching and Learning, Chicago Public Schools, personal interview with Jason Saul, February 13, 2010.

18. "Fast Facts." National Center for Education Statistics. http://nces.ed.gov/fastfacts/display.asp?id=16. (Accessed February 13, 2010.)

19. National Center for Education Statistics. *Achievement Gaps: How Black and White Students in Public Schools Perform in Mathematics and Reading on the National Assessment of Educational Progress*. NCES 2009–455. Washington, D.C.: Institute of Educational Sciences and U.S. Department of Education, July 2009. http://nces.ed.gov/nationsreportcard/pdf/studies/2009455.pdf. (Accessed February 13, 2010.)

20. U.S. Department of Health and Human Services. *Vulnerable Youth and the Transition to Adulthood*. ASPE Research Brief. Washington, D.C: Office of the Assistant Secretary for Planning and Evaluation/Office of Human Services

Policy, July 2009. http://www.urban.org/uploadedpdf/411948 _distressed_neighborhoods.pdf.

21. "Fast Facts." National Center for Education Statistics. http://nces.ed.gov/fastfacts/display.asp?id=372. (Accessed May 17, 2010.)

22. "The Economic Impact of the Achievement Gap in America's Schools." McKinsey & Company, April 2009. http://www.mckinsey.com/App_Media/Images/Page _Images/Offices/SocialSector/PDF/achievement_gap_report .pdf.

23. Nagel, D. "Report: Sweeping Education Reform Needed to Bolster American Competitiveness." *The Journal*, September 10, 2008. http://thejournal.com/Articles/2008/09/10/Report-Sweeping-Education-Reform-Needed-To-Bolster-American-Competitiveness.aspx?Page=1. Citing *21st Century Skills, Education & Competitiveness*, a report sponsored by the Partnership for 21st Century Skills, Ford Motor Company Fund, KnowledgeWorks Foundation, and National Education Association.

24. Wagner, T. *The Global Achievement Gap: Why Even Our Best Schools Don't Teach the New Survival Skills Our Children Need—And What We Can Do About It*. New York: Basic Books, 2008, p. 9.

25. Wagner, *The Global Achievement Gap*.

26. Pink, D. H. *A Whole New Mind*. New York: Penguin Group, 2005.

27. National Center on Education and the Economy. *Tough Choices or Tough Times: The Report of the New Commission on the Skills of the American Workforce*. San Francisco: Jossey-Bass, 2008. See page 15, citing Diana Farrell and Andrew Grant, "China's Looming Talent Shortage," *McKinsey Quarterly*, 2005, No. 4.

28. Guthridge, M., Komm, A. B., and Lawson, E. "Making Talent a Strategic Priority." *McKinsey Quarterly*, January 2008. https://www.mckinseyquarterly.com/Organization/Talent/ Making_talent_a_strategic_priority_2092.

29. Gentleman, A. "'Brain Gain' for India as Elite Return." *The Observer*, April 20, 2008. http://www.guardian.co.uk/ world/2008/apr/20/india.globaleconomy.

30. Holzer, H. J., and Lerman, R. I. "The Future of Middle-Skill Jobs." Brookings Center on Children and Families. *CCF Brief* #41, February 2009. http://www.brookings.edu/~/ media/Files/rc/papers/2009/02_middle_skill_jobs_holzer/02 _middle_skill_jobs_holzer.pdf.

31. Ibid.

32. Ibid.

33. Ibid.

34. Moses, A. R. "Shop Classes Return—with a 21st-Century Twist." *Edutopia*, April 14, 2009. http://www.edutopia.org/ shop-classes-vocational-education-technology. (Accessed February 11, 2010.)

35. National Center for Education Statistics. *Digest of Education Statistics, 2008.* NCES 2009–020. Washington, D.C.: U.S. Department of Education, March 2009. http://nces.ed.gov/ pubsearch/pubsinfo.asp?pubid=2009020. See Chapter Three.

36. Rawe, J. "How Germany Keeps Kids from Dropping Out." *Time*, April 11, 2006. http://www.time.com/time/magazine/ article/0,9171,1182439,00.html.

37. Ibid.

38. Ibid.

39. Holze and Lerman, "The Future of Middle-Skill Jobs."

40. O'Reilly, K. B. "Minority and Women Agents Look to Tap Emerging Markets." *Insurance Journal*, June 23, 2003.

http://www.insurancejournal.com/magazines/southcentral/
2003/06/23/features/30116.htm.

41. Ibid.

42. "FedExperience Pilot Program." The Partnership for Public Service. http://www.ourpublicservice.org/OPS/programs/
fedexperience/.

43. "Developing America's Healthcare IT Expertise." Cisco Systems, 2009. http://www.cisco.com/web/learning/netacad/us/
docs/Healthcare-IT-Networking-Academy.pdf. (Accessed
February 13, 2010.)

Chapter Eight

1. Cohn, J. "What's the One Thing Big Business and the Left
Have in Common?" *New York Times*, April 1, 2007.

2. Ibid.

3. "Who We Are." Coalition to Advance Healthcare Reform.
http://www.coalition4healthcare.org/about/?_c=ymz0mr6m
5yt4uj. (Accessed February 17, 2010.)

4. Rau, J. "Universal Healthcare Gains Unlikely Backer." *Los
Angeles Times*, May 7, 2007.

5. Cohn, "What's the One Thing?"

6. Ibid.

7. Ibid.

8. Rau, "Universal Healthcare Gains Unlikely Backer." See also
Burd, S. A., "How Safeway Is Cutting Health-Care Costs,"
Wall Street Journal, June 12, 2009, p. A15.

9. Burd, "How Safeway Is Cutting Health-Care Costs."

10. Cohn, "What's the One Thing?"

11. Condon, S. "Wal-Mart Supports Health Care Employer Mandate." *CBSNews.com*, July 1, 2009. http://www.cbsnews.com/

blogs/2009/07/01/politics/politicalhotsheet/entry5127536
.shtml. (Accessed February 17, 2010.)

12. Cohn, "What's the One Thing?"

13. Rau, "Universal Healthcare Gains Unlikely Backer."

14. Cohn, "What's the One Thing?"

15. Peterson, K., and Pfitzer, M. "Lobbying for Good." *Stanford Social Innovation Review*, 2009, 7(1), 44–49.

16. Carney, E. N. "What You Don't See." *National Journal*, March 21, 2008. http://news.nationaljournal.com/articles/080321nj2.htm. (Accessed February 17, 2010.)

17. Igan, D., Mishra, P., and Tressel, T. "A Fistful of Dollars: Lobbying and the Financial Crisis." Working Paper. *International Monetary Fund*, December 2009. http://www.imf.org/external/pubs/ft/wp/2009/wp09287.pdf.

18. *2010 Congressional Pig Book*. Citizens Against Government Waste, 2010. http://www.cagw.org/reports/pig-book/2010/.

19. Cramer, A. "Business and Government: Working Together in the Reset World." *BSR Insight*, July 14, 2009.

20. Adamy, J., and Zimmerman, A. "Wal-Mart Backs Drive to Make Companies Pay for Health Coverage." *Wall Street Journal*, July 1, 2009, p. A1.

21. Ibid.

22. Bonini, S.M.J., Mendonca, L. T., and Oppenheim, J. M. "When Social Issues Become Strategic." *McKinsey Quarterly*, 2006, No. 2. http://www.sdgrantmakers.org/whso06.pdf. (Accessed February 17, 2010.)

23. Di Meglio, F. "B-School Students with a Cause." *BusinessWeek*, January 6, 2005. http://www.businessweek.com/bschools/content/jan2005/bs2005016_5334_bs001.htm. (Accessed February 16, 2010.)

24. Burd, "How Safeway Is Cutting Health-Care Costs."

25. Donovan, W. "Full Contact Investing: Active Shareholders Get Engaged." *About.com*. http://socialinvesting.about.com/od/srishareholders/a/socialactivism.htm. (Accessed February 17, 2010.)

26. Janet Burton, senior director, Ronald McDonald House Charities, personal interview with Jason Saul, March 30, 2010.

27. Ibid.

28. Backaler, J. "KFC's Success in China: An Interview with Warren Liu, Former VP of Yum! Brands Greater China." Joel Backaler's Instablog, July 1, 2009. http://seekingalpha .com/instablog/339769-joel-backaler/10822-kfcs-success-in-china-an-interview-with-warren-liu-former-vp-of-yum-brands-greater-china.

29. "Governor Kaine Announces Partnership to Improve Citizen Access to GED Content." Literacy Council of North Virginia. http://www.lcnv.org/docs/ged_ondemand.pdf. (Accessed February 17, 2010.)

30. List, J. "SC Johnson and USAID Partner to Increase Pyrethrum Production in Rwanda." *Alliance Innovations: Newsletter of the Global Development Alliance*, USAID, Summer 2009, p. 8. http://www.usaid.gov/our_work/global_partnerships/gda/newsletter/summer2009.pdf. (Accessed February 17, 2010.)

31. "GE Eyes $1.5 Billion in Cleantech Research by 2010." *Reuters*, May 27, 2009. http://www.reuters.com/article/idUSTRE54 Q0NG20090527.

32. General Electric. "Healthymagination." http://www.healthy magination.com/.

33. Ibid.

34. Bhattacharya, C. B., and Sen, S. "Doing Better at Doing Good: When, Why, and How Consumers Respond to Corporate

Social Initiatives." *California Management Review*, 2004, 47(2), 9–24.

35. Dutton, G. "How Nike Is Changing the World, One Factory at a Time." *Ethisphere*, March 26, 2008. http://ethisphere.com/how-nike-is-changing-the-world-one-factory-at-a-time/.

Chapter Nine

1. Bonini, S., Brun, N., and Rosenthal, M. "Valuing Corporate Social Responsibility." *McKinsey Quarterly*, February 2009.

2. Friscia, T. "The 2009 Clinton Global Initiative: Corporate Social Capitalism Is the New Basis of Global Competition." *AMR Research*, October 2, 2009. http://www.amrresearch.com/content/view.aspx?compURI=tcm:7-48415.

3. Frederick, J. "Walgreens Offers New Urban Solution: Expanded Grocery Set for 'Food Deserts.'" *Drug Store News*, June 29, 2009.

Chapter Eleven

1. Berk, C. C. "Pepsi's Gamble: Sitting on Sidelines at the Super Bowl." CNBC.com, December 17, 2009. http://www.cnbc.com/id/34465594. (Accessed February 27, 2010.)

2. Hodge, S. A. "U.S. States Lead the World in High Corporate Taxes." Tax Foundation, March 18, 2008. http://www.taxfoundation.org/publications/show/22917.html. (Accessed February 27, 2010.)

3. Blodgett, H. "The Conscientious Investor." *Atlantic Monthly*, December 2007.

4. Goldman Sachs, "Introducing GS Sustain" (see chap. 12, n. 12).

5. Basil Demeroutis, personal interview with Jason Saul, March 1, 2010.

6. Independent Sector. "Facts and Figures About Charitable Organizations." Fact sheet, October 30, 2009. http://www.independentsector.org/programs/research/Charitable_Fact_Sheet.pdf. (Accessed March 30, 2010.)

7. Based on analysis of Urban Institute National Program Classification Codes. http://nccs.urban.org/classification/NPC.cfm. (Accessed February 27, 2010.)

8. McNichol, E., and Johnson, N. "Recession Continues to Batter State Budgets; State Responses Could Slow Recovery." Center on Budget and Policy Priorities, February 25, 2010. http://www.cbpp.org/cms/index.cfm?fa=view&id=711. (Accessed February 27, 2010.)

9. "Survey: Most Americans Believe Government Broken." CNN *Politics*, February 22, 2010. http://www.cnn.com/2010/POLITICS/02/21/poll.broken.govt/index.html. (Accessed February 27, 2010.)

10. Reich, R. B. *SuperCapitalism: The Transformation of Business, Democracy, and Everyday Life*. New York: Knopf, 2007, pp. 182–184.

Acknowledgments

S*ocial Innovation, Inc.* was made possible by the many corporate, foundation, and government clients of my firm, Mission Measurement, who believed in the power of measurement and the possibility of business. In particular, I want to thank the early believers and first friends, among them Janet Burton at McDonald's/RMHC; Amina Dickerson at Kraft Foods; Brad Googins and Cheryl Kiser, formerly of Boston College Center for Corporate Citizenship; Jason McBriarty at Levi Strauss & Co.; Kristi Ragan at DAI; Mats Lederhausen at be Cause; Michelle Stegall at Walmart; Paula Berezin at Social Capital Partners; Marlene Ibsen at Travelers Foundation; and Charlie Moore at the Committee Encouraging Corporate Philanthropy. Thank you for believing in me and my work.

I also want to thank the talented staff of Mission Measurement, many of whom inspired my thinking, refined it, and challenged it. Erin Simmons, my first "campaign manager," was an amazing thought-partner without whom I would never have pulled this off. My partner Pranav Kothari provided valuable early input as well as the "air cover" I needed to complete this book. My colleague Cheryl Davenport helped me to "ground-truth" these principles in the field with our clients, and Wendy Lazar helped me to quarterback this project all the way to the goal line.

The project team for this book was world-class. My agent, Carol Mann, helped me to conceptualize this project and make it a reality, and my editor at Jossey-Bass, Karen Murphy, believed in this project from day one and went way above and beyond to make it a better book. My developmental editor, Sachin Waikar, basically served as my copilot from beginning to end, helping me to structure and write this book. And my dogged research assistants, Hillary Harnett and Melanie Halverson, hunted down case studies and sources with great dispatch and reliability.

I owe my biggest thanks to my family, and particularly to my wife, Lisa, who gave birth to our second son at the same time I gave birth to my second book. This book was first conceived on our honeymoon, and Lisa's patience, support, love, and dedication to me and my vision made this book possible.

Finally, I want to thank all of the innovative companies and leading practitioners whom I interviewed for this project; you are the real authors of this book.

About the Author

J ason Saul is one of the nation's leading experts on measuring social impact. He is the founder and CEO of Mission Measurement LLC, a strategy consulting firm that helps corporations, nonprofits, and public sector clients to measure and improve their social impact. He has advised some of the world's largest corporations, government agencies, and nonprofits, including Walmart, McDonald's, Kraft Foods, Levi Strauss & Co., Easter Seals, American Red Cross, the Smithsonian, and the U.S. Agency for International Development.

Jason serves on the faculty of Northwestern's Kellogg School of Management, where he teaches corporate social responsibility and nonprofit management. He also serves on the faculty of Boston College's Center for Corporate Citizenship. He is the author of numerous books and articles on social strategy and measurement, including *Benchmarking for Nonprofits: How to Manage, Measure and Improve Performance* (Fieldstone Press, 2006) and *The End of Fundraising: How to Sell Your Impact in an Era of Outcomes* (forthcoming from Jossey-Bass in February 2011).

Jason holds a J.D. from the University of Virginia School of Law, an M.P.P. from Harvard University's John F. Kennedy School of Government, and a B.A. from Cornell University. Jason was awarded the Harry S. Truman Scholarship for leadership and public service, and has been recognized by Crain's Chicago Business as a "40 under 40" business leader and by *Bloomberg Businessweek* as one of America's Most Promising Social Entrepreneurs.

Index